W. H. AUDEN

Complete list of titles in the series available from the publisher on request.

W. H. AUDEN

Wendell Stacy Johnson

A Frederick Ungar Book
CONTINUUM • NEW YORK

1990

The Continuum Publishing Company
370 Lexington Avenue
New York, NY 10017

Printed in the United States of America

Library of Congress Cataloging-in-Publication Data

Johnson, Wendell Stacy, 1927–
    W.H. Auden / Wendell Stacy Johnson.
        p.   cm. — (Literature and life. British writers)
    "A Frederick Ungar book."
    Bibliography: p.
    Includes index.
    ISBN 0–8264–0449–9
    1. Auden, W. H. (Wystan Hugh), 1907–1973. 2. Poets, English—
20th century—Biography. I. Title. II. Series.
PR6001.U4Z755   1990
811'.52—dc20
[B]   89–32282
                                                                          CIP

To the Memory of Arlow Fielding Hill

Contents

Preface

This book is based upon a reading of and a personal acquaintance with its subject. Its aim is to introduce the general reader and the student to Auden's life and work, and to arrive at a critical estimate of that work.

My thanks are due to a number of friends and colleagues for their help. I am grateful to Don Bachardy, executor of the Christopher Isherwood estate, for kindly allowing me to go through and make notes upon the very large Isherwood collection of Auden manuscripts, typescripts, and letters; to Professor Charles Matz for his meticulous reading of my text; to Professor Richard Katz for help and encouragement; to Dr. Lola Szladits, Curator of the Berg Collection of the New York Public Library, whose rich holdings of Auden material I have been allowed to consult; to the staff of the Houghton Library of Harvard University. I must acknowledge special indebtedness to Professor Edward Mendelson, Auden's critic, biographer, editor, and literary executor, for generous aid on point after point.

All passages from the author's work—poetry, drama, letters, and criticism—are cited by permission of the estate of W. H. Auden.

Southampton, New York
January 1989

Chronology

1907   February 21: Born at York, third son of Dr. George Auden and Constance Bicknell Auden; christened Wystan Hugh Auden.

1908   Family moves to Solihull, on the outskirts of Birmingham, Dr. Auden having been appointed medical officer for the city schools and professor of public health at the University of Birmingham.

1915   Autumn: Enrolls at St. Edmund's School, in Surrey, where he meets Christopher Isherwood; a precocious boy, he excels at science.

1920   Leaves preparatory school to enter Gresham's School at Holt, a small minor public school that specializes in the sciences; his ambition is to be a mining engineer, but he also studies biology, begins to read Freud, acts in school plays, and wins prizes for Latin composition.

1922   Winter: Realizes that he has lost his childhood faith, and publishes his first poem in the school magazine.

1925   Summer: European travel with his father; Autumn: Enters Christ Church College, Oxford, where he studies natural science, along with politics, economics, and some philosophy, incidentally studying literature with Nevill Coghill, by whom he is so impressed that he takes English at last as his subject, and Coghill as his tutor.

1928   Summer: His friend Stephen Spender prints privately the first volume of Auden's poems; Spender's press breaks down and the last stages in producing the forty or fifty

11

copies are taken over by a professional printer. Autumn: Goes to Berlin to spend a year learning German as well as working at new poetry.

1929 Tutoring in London.

1930 Schoolmaster at Larchfield Academy, a boy's school in Scotland, near Glasgow.

1930 First professionally published volume, *Poems,* accepted for Faber by T. S. Eliot, appears in paperback with a pale blue cover; most of the volume consists of the play *Paid on Both Sides.*

1932 Begins teaching at the Downs School, Colwall; *The Orators,* largely about teaching, teachers, and students, is published.

1933 June: Experiences a quasi-religious sense, while talking with friends on a lawn, of being "invaded" by a power that allowed him to know what it is to "love one's neighbour as oneself"; this may, long before experiences in Spain and in New York, signal the beginning of a movement back to Christianity.
A second edition of *Poems* appears, with changes and additions; *The Dance of Death,* published and performed by the Group Theatre.

1934 First American volume of *Poems,* including *The Orators,* and *The Dance of Death,* published by Random House, the firm that remains his American publisher throughout his life (as Faber remains his British publisher); his reputation in the United States grows from this time.

1935 May: Publication of *The Dog Beneath the Skin* (written in collaboration with Isherwood), which is performed by the Group Theatre. June: At the suggestion of Isherwood, who was asked first, marries Erika Mann, daughter of Thomas Mann, in order to give her British citizenship and safety from Nazi persecution; it is a casual Registry Office marriage, and the two see each other only intermittently afterward.

Autumn: Leaves teaching to write for films at the General Post Office Film Unit in London.

1936 July to September: With Louis MacNeice, travels to and about Iceland, which the Audens regard as their ancestral home. Auden's and Isherwood's *Ascent of F6* published (to be performed the following year by the Group Theatre). Autumn: *Look, Stranger!* (not Auden's own choice for a title) published.

1937 Winter: Journey to Spain, to do propaganda work for the Loyalists; shocked to discover that the churches are closed. Meets Charles Williams and is impressed by his "personal sanctity." The shocking discovery and this meeting have been taken as presaging Auden's return to religion. Summer: *Letters from Iceland* published.

1938 Travels to China and returns by way of the United States, with Isherwood, crossing America by train to New York; they are greeted as literary celebrities. Autumn: *On the Frontier,* a collaboration with Isherwood, published and performed, once more by the Group Theatre.

1939 Returns to America, to stay. Early spring: Auden and Isherwood's *Journey to a War* published. Mid-spring: meets Chester Kallman. This is the beginning of a lifelong relationship.

1940 Publishes *Another Time,* teaches at the New School; returns to Anglican Christianity, beginning regularly to attend and receive the Eucharist in the Episcopal Church.

1941 March: Publication of *The Double Man* (in England, *New Year Letter*). May: *Paul Bunyan* performed at Columbia University. Summer teaching at Olivet College. Autumn: Teaching at University of Michigan, Ann Arbor.

1942 Autumn, winter, and early spring: Teaches at Swarthmore College; summer on Fire Island.

1944 *For the Time Being* (including "The Sea and the Mirror") published.

1945 April: *Collected Poetry* appears. Spring and summer: In Europe for the Strategic Bombing Survey as a civilian but with a form of military rank; visits England.

1946 Teaches at Bennington College; becomes a United States citizen; returns in the autumn to teaching at the New School.

1947 Teaches part-time at Barnard College. *The Age of Anxiety* published in July.

1948 Summer: Lives in rented house on Ischia.

1949 Lectures at the University of Virginia, the lectures to be published the following year as *The Enchafèd Flood*.

1950 *Collected Shorter Poems* published in England, with verse from 1930 to 1944. Autumn: Lectures at Mount Holyoke College.

1951 Publication of *Nones;* premiere of *The Rake's Progress* at Teatro Fenice, Venice.

1953 Late summer: Moves to 77 St. Mark's Place, in Manhattan's Bowery district; winter and spring: William Allan Neilson Professor at Smith College (a visiting professorship that includes the giving of two or three lectures and presence on the campus).

1955 Winter: *The Shield of Achilles* appears.

1956 Becomes professor of poetry at Oxford; his inaugural lecture, *Making, Knowing and Judging,* is published.

1958 Moves from Ischia to Kirchstetten, Austria, for a summer residence; the move is marked by his poetic farewell, "Good-Bye to the Mezzogiorno."

1960 *Homage to Clio* is published.

1961 *Elegy for Young Lovers* presented in Stuttgart, the libretto a collaboration with Chester Kallman.

1962 Autumn: *The Dyer's Hand,* a collection of critical essays and lectures, is published.

1964 Returns to Iceland for a brief visit and to Berlin, on a Ford Foundation program.

1965 *About the House* appears.

1966 Summer: *The Bassarids,* an Auden-Kallman collaboration based on the *Bacchae* of Euripides, with music by Henze, presented in Salzburg.

1968 *Secondary Worlds* is published.

1969 *City Without Walls* is published.

1970 *A Certain World,* Auden's selection of favorite literary passages, is published.

1971 *Academic Graffiti.*

1972 *Epistle to a Godson* appears; Auden returns to Oxford, to live at Christ Church.

1973 The Auden-Kallman *Love's Labour's Lost,* with music by Nicholas Nabokov, is produced in Brussels. *Forewords and Afterwords* is published. September: Wystan Hugh Auden dies in Vienna, and is buried in the Kirchstetten graveyard.

W. H. Auden

1

Poet

Just before W. H. Auden died in September 1973, he was widely regarded as the greatest poet writing in English. It was a judgment that had been disputed. Some readers and some critics found him too flippant to be taken seriously. He indulged in wisecracks and in vulgar slang while writing about tragic death and divine love. He was perverse. He called Tennyson "the stupidest English poet," although he consciously echoed Tennyson and privately admitted that he was also one of the greatest English poets. He declared that the Christian doctrine of the Atonement was abominable. Yet he was, at last, a devout Christian who believed in messianic suffering and salvation, if not in the legalistic language of the Calvinist covenant. He contradicted himself. He was messy. He teased people. He gave parties in his New York Bowery apartment to which he invited theologians, priests, male prostitutes, gentlewomen, celebrated artists and actresses, and ordinary drunks. They usually had a good time. (Hermione Gingold, however, that marvelously funny comedienne, was not amused when the grand Dame Edith Sitwell marched out wearing Miss Gingold's mink and leaving behind Dame Edith's ratty squirrel.)

Auden enjoyed the fame and fortune he finally earned, but they never made him feel grand. He was more excited by meeting Greta Garbo—at photographer Cecil Beaton's studio—than by earning any literary award or visiting professorship. When two college students sat across from him, riding downtown from Hunter College on the Lexington

Avenue IRT, and one whispered to the other, "That man looks just like W. H. Auden, but he couldn't be, could he?" he leaned across, smiling, and loudly said, "My dear, it is." He was as pleased then as he was to discover that the rector of St. Mark's Church in the Bowery, which he regularly attended, was, as he said, "a fan." He never altogether grew up, nor did he want to. When told that he simply had to fold up his clothes and pack his bag before flying to Europe, he could sulk and reply in a baby's voice, "Mother should do it for me." At the same time, he was the most adult and morally responsible of men. His sense of moral responsibility haunted him. He was committed to order, to law, in the highest and least trivial sense of those terms. For him, moral order and the order of art were not at all separate.

At Oxford, in the various American college towns where he camped out, in New York where he inhabited a cold-water flat in a slum building, he lived in chaos, a chaos of papers, books, clothes, dirty ashtrays, and dirty dishes, all strewn about in shocking disarray. His bed was never made, and in cold weather it was covered not with blankets but with coats and miscellaneous garments; its legs were likely to be missing, and the whole thing propped up with ancient phone books. A friend, in despair, once asked him, "Can't you keep any sort of order in your life?" He replied merely, "Yes, in my poetry."

Law and order were for him his poetic achievement. His poem "Law like Love" begins with a reference to the gardener, and that is his recurring metaphor to express the poet's task: to make a garden of disorder, or, in the language of his elegy on Yeats, to "make a vineyard of the curse."

He could be perverse and messy or serious, in order, without worrying about what people thought of him, because, as he said, he knew who he was. Who was he?

Wystan Hugh Auden was born February 21, 1907, in York, England. The youngest of three boys, he remained close to all his family, his father, a medical doctor, his strong-minded mother, and his brothers. His unusual Christian name was that of a ninth-century saint, and his almost equally odd family name may be of Scandinavian origin; like his father, Wystan Auden believed that the family was descended from Icelandic ancestors.[1]

When he was less than two years old, the Audens moved to a village near Birmingham, where Dr. Auden became school medical officer. The boy read scientific books for pleasure, along with fantasy and other fiction. He was interested in engineering, and he especially loved old factories, mines, and mining equipment. His fascination for the scientific and mechanical showed something of his father's influence, and yet more of his Uncle Harry's, for the uncle was an industrial chemist. Auden's mother was, at the same time, equally influential. She was a lover of music and a staunch high-church Anglican; both the poet's lifelong interest in musical forms, the opera in particular, later, and his return in middle age to the Anglican communion, he could ascribe in part to her. In childhood and early adolescence, however, he cherished the ambition of being not a musician or a priest or a poet but a mining engineer.

In 1915 the eight-year-old Wystan went to St. Edmund's boarding school, in Surrey. He was a remarkably composed and clever lad who talked surprisingly like an adult. One of his several school nicknames was "Witty." The absence of his father during the years of World War I was, he believed, significant in his emotional development. It was his mother who cared for him, tried to teach him (about sex, a matter that he already understood fairly well), and was in some ways his model. In 1917 he formed a close friendship with a fellow student aged thirteen, Christopher Isherwood, and that friendship, virtually as strong as a family tie, was to be maintained throughout his life. Isherwood was at first amused by the younger boy with ink-stained fingers and a face as white as pudding; he became Auden's confidant and best critic.

Although barely failing to win a scholarship, Auden went to Gresham's School in Norfolk when he was himself thirteen. There he studied literature, especially poetry, began to lose his religious faith, and formed with a fellow student another close attachment, one more intense than his relationship to Isherwood, but an attachment that did not last so long. The boy, Robert Medley, did, even so, make a lasting difference in Wystan Auden's life. One day when the two were talking about their futures, Medley casually asked him, "Tell me, do you write poetry?" The fifteen-year-old Auden replied that he never had, and suddenly he knew that this was just what he wanted to do. His delight in rock formations, in old mines and mining machinery, had been a poetic response to their mystery, power, and beauty. The would-be mining engineer was transformed into a writer.

In 1922, Auden was writing poems about landscape, seasons, and times of day, as he would continue to do for many years. He was reading, too, the poetry of Walter de la Mare, Thomas Hardy, and Robert Frost. At the same time, he continued to follow his bent for science, now including botany, chemistry, and zoology. He was never to believe that his various interests over the years, in science, politics, psychology, religion, and poetry, belonged in separate compartments. As for the poetry, his first piece to be printed was "Woods in the Rain," which Michael Davidson—who was as much interested in the boy as in his writing—included in the 1924 volume of *Public School Verse*. It was a very minor effort even for a boy of seventeen, and the young poet's name was misprinted as "W. H. Arden."

When he left school to go on to Oxford, Auden called himself an "anarchist individualist." It was in 1925 that he entered Christ Church, one of the largest of Oxford colleges; there he joined the Musical Union, studied biology, made new friends, and became in both his life and his poetry much less an anarchistic individual and much more a social creature. As Edward Mendelson observes, the young man felt the appeal of two traditions, that of "vatic" poetry and that of "civic" poetry.[2] The vatic note is intensely personal, original, and visionary—expressing a private vision—in contrast with the civic intention to address oneself to public and moral purposes. After struggling for some time, Auden chose to write not "modernist" and often inaccessible poetry but contemporary and deliberately public verse. The beginning of his serious concern for the society around him was in those Oxford years. He tried at Oxford to avoid the Romantic pose of an aesthete. He also abandoned completely his parents' religious beliefs (or thought he did) as he gave up his sense of sexual guilt (or thought he did). He was increasingly sympathetic with social movements, and he supported the General Strike of 1926, although not so actively as some of his friends had. Yet, in spite of his generally left-wing sympathies, in all such matters he was not totally committed to one theory or position. The early Auden, that is, from his late teens to his late twenties, has sometimes been thought of as a Marxist or a Freudian, or both. He drew upon Marx, Freud, and other thinkers, but he was never a "church-going" member of one school any more than he was at that point a church-going Christian.

Although he was specializing in the sciences while at Oxford—at least, to begin with—he persuaded a young don at Exeter College, Nevill Coghill, to tutor him in English literature. From him and from Charles Wrenn Auden learned about Old English poetry, and his fascination with that difficult language and its forms was deepened when he heard the lectures of J. R. R. Tolkien, the University Professor of Anglo-Saxon. Coghill, Wrenn, and Tolkien were, or were to become, celebrated scholars and writers. Some years later, Auden would be one of the warmest admirers of Tolkien's Hobbit stories, especially *The Lord of the Rings,* with its linguistic playfulness, imaginative geography, and fascinating maps. He especially liked Jane Austen and Trollope, and he could quote long passages from Dickens, but Auden was mainly interested in poetry ancient and modern, in-

cluding that of Herbert, Pope, and Dryden—even though,
or perhaps in part because, the first was deeply religious,
and the other two were then quite out of fashion. He was
rarely bothered by what others believed he ought to read
and like. He enjoyed detective stories, was bored by Wordsworth, and did not care much for Romantic poetry or
most modern novels. He thought that every college student
should know a number of languages, a body of poetry (by
heart), mathematics, geology, archaeology, church liturgy,
farming—and cooking. He did not, however, cook.

A fellow Christ Church student, radical, and homosexual, Tom Driberg, introduced him to the poetry of T. S.
Eliot, who was to be an important person in Auden's life—
years later, he referred to Eliot as "Daddy"—but not, for
his poetry, a major or a lasting influence. Auden was a vo-
racious reader of American as well as British verse, Emily
Dickinson and Frost as well as Gerard Manley Hopkins
and Hardy. He was now himself writing regularly and producing a good deal of poetry, much of it to be rejected or,
at least not published. Some was, however, printed, as early
as 1925, in a volume of *Oxford Poetry*, which included
much less competent writing by Graham Greene, Cecil Day-
Lewis, A. L. Rowse, and Harold Acton. Day-Lewis soon became, along with Stephen Spender and Isherwood (who had
already left Cambridge), one of Auden's closest friends and
associates in poetry and in private life. There were other
good friends, including John Betjeman, the witty high-
church lad who loved Victorian Gothic buildings and who
would much later be named poet laureate; Rex Warner,
poet and athlete; and W. L. McElwee, with whom Auden
was briefly but intensely in love.

In June 1927, on the advice of Sacheverell Sitwell, the
twenty-year-old undergraduate submitted a group of poems
to Faber, T. S. Eliot's publisher. Eliot read them, and after
three months' delay, for which he apologized, wrote to the
young man that his verses were not yet right for publication, but that he was interested in following Auden's work.

From Eliot, these could be taken as words of encouragement; and Auden was encouraged.

In 1927, too, he and Day-Lewis edited that year's volume of *Oxford Poetry,* including work by Driberg and Warner, by Louis MacNeice, and (anonymously printed, since the author was not an Oxford man) by Isherwood. That summer, Auden and his father spent several weeks in Yugoslavia. When he returned to England, the burgeoning poet wrote "The Watershed," a lyric that suggests his sense of how this time was, in fact, a turning point or watershed in his life—he was now on the verge of a literary career.

It was to be a literary rather than a mainly academic career. Nineteen twenty-eight was his last year at Oxford. When he took his final examinations that summer, he surprised friends and acquaintances—including J. I. M. Stewart, the scholar, critic, and later (writing as Michael Innes) writer of donnish thrillers—by receiving only a third-class Honours degree. His was not a conventionally academic mind, and he might have consoled himself by recalling other poets who had done little better: Matthew Arnold, tutored by Wordsworth, gained a second-class degree. More important, 1928 was when his first volume of poetry was published. It was privately printed, by Spender on his own press, which broke down so that the final pages and the binding had to be done commercially. It sold no copies at all. Still, W. H. Auden was a poet in print.

He was writing almost constantly and becoming more self-critical. The drafts of poetry that he wrote in Berlin during 1928 and 1929 were largely canceled and remained mostly unpublished.[3] They suggest a young writer who is not yet sure about his style; they also reveal an odd and impressive flair for phrase along with formal control.

Auden's Berlin year, financed by his parents, was an unsettling as well as an exhilarating time. Some accounts of his choosing that city for the year abroad have stressed the appeal of its sexual freedom and its advanced music and theatre. Auden himself, however, ascribed his choice not to

these but simply to the facts that, bored with French culture, he was not drawn to Paris, while he could not tolerate
living in Rome because of Mussolini, then a firmly established dictator, as Hitler was yet to become. This was, still,
the Berlin of the playwright Bertolt Brecht, and Brecht's
sometime collaborator, the composer Kurt Weill. It was
also the Berlin of the rising Nazi party, of anti-Semitic riots
and other acts of violence, some committed by the far left
but more, and more menacingly, by the Fascist right. The
disturbed mood of the place and time is represented by
Christopher Isherwood, who joined Auden there in 1929,
in his semifictional *Berlin Stories*. That book and the dramatic and musical versions of it, *I Am a Camera* and *Cab-
aret*, reveal corruption and fear that are as pervasive as the
vitality, the indulgence, and the artistic and sexual experi-
menting of the young and not-so-young, the creative and
the self-destructive.

It was in this feverish environment that Wystan Auden
took up the ideas of his new friend John Layard. Layard
had been a disciple of the American psychiatrist Homer
Lane, whose ideas he fully accepted, extended, and
exaggerated.[4] According to Layard, all disease could be explained not merely by neurosis but by faults of character: a
sore throat is the symptom of lying ("the liar's quinsy," Auden terms the complaint in a line from "Petition"—as it
would later be entitled—written at this time); those who
suffer back pain carry a burden of guilt; and so on. Apparently Auden took these explanations quite literally at first,
although Layard's ideas, like the poet's supposed Marxism
and the memories of his Christian faith, were to become
convenient tropes as much as true convictions. That he continued to be fascinated by the link between illness and
moral character is, however, apparent in much of his writing through the thirties, including his "Letter to a Wound."

If Auden felt a weakness in his own character at that moment and in that ominous place, it was simply his homosexuality. He was never very promiscuous or even passionately
sexual, and he probably seemed as tame as most other En-

glishmen to some of the wilder Berliners. But he felt during these years some anxious doubt about the social and moral rightness of his sexual nature. Interestingly, it was only after his reconversion to Christianity that he could accept his inclination. He would then acknowledge that homosexual acts were sinful—and continue to practice them. He accepted the (Anglican) belief that all persons sin and all can be forgiven. Now, in his early twenties and without such a belief, he had no such comfort.

One part of Auden's life that he took more seriously than some commentators have supposed was teaching. He was, in several senses, a teaching poet. His poems and his essays on poetry inform, and even provide pointed morals. For a good part of his adult life, too, he taught in schools and colleges. To begin with, his teaching was a matter of chance. He wrote from Berlin to a friend, in 1929, that he was looking for a job and was willing to do anything, including burglary. But when, in 1930, Day-Lewis left his post at Larchfield Academy, a boy's school in Scotland, Wystan Auden applied for the position and was accepted. He was surprised to discover that he enjoyed the profession, which he followed for the next five years, and to which he would later return as a college lecturer. His "schoolmastering" was sometimes earnestly undertaken, but he was capable of doing comic turns in the classroom, too. He believed that teachers should be clowns as well as mentors.

While he was at Larchfield, his verses were accepted by T. S. Eliot, to be published by Faber in the 1930 volume entitled simply *Poems*. At the same time he began writing book reviews for major literary journals, and he was trying his hand at playwriting; his charade, *Paid on Both Sides*, takes up half of the 1930 collection. No other play of his from this period survives (parts and revisions of them appearing only in later work).[5]

The teacher-poet-reviewer was himself reviewed after the 1930 volume appeared, and not altogether favorably. Both the *Times Literary Supplement* and *The Listener* found his poetry peculiar and obscure. The poet was distressed. Unlike some other writers of the day, he regarded obscurity as a serious fault.

Yet the young Auden could be eccentric in speech, in behavior, and, perhaps more than he realized, in writing. He attacked Edward Upward's religious interests and wrote a parody of Anglican litany, with all-knowing God replaced by Agatha Christie's all-seeing detective—"O Poirot, deliver us"—even though he had just revised and published his own essentially religious poem, the one later entitled "Petition," that begins with an address to God, "Sir, no man's enemy." He seemed unpredictable, even perverse. Before emerging from a train when Upward was to meet him, he put on a false red beard (Upward was not at the station, and he had to take it off); he played outrageous tricks on friends and students alike.

A short time after suffering from an anal fistula ("stigmata of Sodom," he said, perhaps jokingly, but still with Layard's ideas in mind), he wrote the "Letter to a Wound," finding psychological and moral meaning in an injury but doing so in an impudently physical way. The wound poem was intended for inclusion in what emerges as *The Orators,* Auden's "memorial," as he first planned it, to the recently dead D. H. Lawrence. Yet the work parodies Lawrence, as well as Eliot and Stein. While Auden largely agreed with Lawrence that psychosomatic illness prevents union of mind and body, he gave an oddly comic note to this agreement. He said that true poetry came from the penis, not the intellect.

Ultimately, the author did not consider his *Orators* Lawrentian. He had to conclude that any person's enemy is that person's own weakness. And weakness could only be revealed as laughable if it was to be cured. He declared that in his times one could write nothing but comic poetry, "real slapstick."

By late 1931, the young teacher had decided that Larchfield Academy was in decline. He was, in any event, en-

gaged in a love affair with a young man with whom he
spent some time in the Shetland Islands. He was also meeting interesting people and making friends in Scotland. One
of them, Anne Fremantle, with whom he discussed religion,
remained a friend throughout his life. He failed to tell her,
in their discussions, that he had abandoned his Christian
beliefs. This was, in fact, a period when he lacked almost
any anchoring beliefs, except, perhaps, a belief in family,
friends, and self. He was rapidly growing away from the
influence of Layard and that of Lawrence. True, he was impressed by the "scientific humanism" of Gerald Heard, an
author, editor, student of science, and (perhaps this was a
part of his appeal) a happily adjusted homosexual. To
Heard Auden addressed his 1932 poem "A Happy New
Year." That influence, however, lasted only briefly. And the
poet's flirtation with orthodox Marxism, at this point
when many of his friends were declaring themselves Communists, was tenuous and transient. His skepticism about
politics and politicians qualified even his supposedly proletarian poetry, although he could declare as late as 1935
that Marx, like Freud, was "right," adding that Communism and Christianity held to identical views on the equal-
ity of all persons. Still, he knew already in 1932 that he
was " a bourgeois" and would not join the Party.

In that year he finally left Larchfield. He spent the summer in London, living with Robert Medley, now pursuing
his career as a painter, and the theatrical director Rupert
Doone, meeting and chatting with Edith Sitwell (who found
his poetry uninteresting), and looking for another teaching
job. By September, he had found one: He went to Colwall,
a village between Worcester and Wales, to teach boys aged
ten to thirteen at the Downs School. Although he taught a
variety of subjects, from French to biology, he concentrated
on English literature and he started a school magazine to
encourage young writers. The students found him unpredictable and often very funny; they called him "Uncle
Wiz." The Downs School had a Quaker background and

flourished in part because of the headmaster's wife's being a Cadbury chocolate heiress—or so Auden thought. Perversely, although he liked the school, the boys, the master and his wife, he wrote to Iris Snodgrass that he was "homesick" for Larchfield.

He was now writing verse that used odd forms, in particular the Anglo-Saxon line with its pronounced alliteration, to describe very modern people and situations. Odd as it was, that verse was beginning to be widely admired by 1933, when the anthology *New Country* was published, including his work along with that of his friends Isherwood, Upward, Rex Warner, Day-Lewis, and Charles Madge. The latter two contributed writing that praised Auden by name. People began now to speak of these young men as "the Auden group," often taking it to be a coterie of like-minded— vaguely Communist—poets and critics, even though the various members of the so-called group were quite dissimilar, as Geoffrey Grigson observed, and even though Auden was not a Communist. Yet, for some years, Auden, Isherwood, Day-Lewis, and Spender were to be lumped together not only as close friends but as a "school."

Auden's only school was in fact the school where he taught, and he continued to like it. Now twenty-six, he soon fell in love with a young man, considerably younger than himself but not a student, for Auden would not allow himself to have erotic relations with boys in his charge; and he wrote love poetry, more free and open than that which he had earlier penned. He made friends with his fellow teachers, sang in a school choir, got a car and drove it carelessly, and learned—for the first time, he said—to love his neighbor as himself. He did not yet regard himself as a religious person, certainly not as a believer, but he was already on the way to reconversion if only in the sense that he could regret his snobbery and selfishness and could write about the primacy of love: love for friends, sexual love, family love, and love of humankind. He was becoming a lyric poet.

Even so, his *Dance of Death*, a musical verse play and ballet written in collaboration with Medley and Doone and presented at last in 1934, was a wry, deliberately slapdash, and not at all romantically lyric piece of work. Personally and poetically, it seemed, Wystan Auden was still in transition from skepticism to moral certainty, from assumed manner to assured style.

During the years 1934 and 1935, he combined his interests in teaching, drama, and poetry, first by producing a medieval play about the Flood in Genesis, in which he spoke the voice of God, and then by editing, with John Garrett, an anthology of verse lyric, dramatic, and comic, which included jingles and biblical passages along with lines from Eliot, Lawrence, and Vachel Lindsay. It was called *The Poet's Tongue,* and it was well received and often used in schools.

The plays he wrote in this period were "The Reformatory," "The Enemies of the Bishop," "The Fronny," "In the Year of My Youth," and then "The Chase," which included elements from those earlier attempts—the attempts that survive if at all only in fragmentary form. Even "The Chase," as submitted for publication, did not appear in print; it was accepted by Faber, but the author himself soon expressed doubts, and, conferring with Christopher Isherwood in Copenhagen, decided that the two should collaborate on a complete revision. The result at last of all these efforts was the Auden-Isherwood play *The Dog Beneath the Skin* (1935). This is a fantastic drama that deals with war, Fascism, and both mental and moral derangement. It received largely unenthusiastic reviews.

In 1935, Wystan Auden, who was having sexual relations with a young gardener at the Downs School, and whose homosexuality was known to friends, family, and some colleagues, married.

His bride was Erika Mann, the daughter of Thomas Mann, the German novelist. Threatened by the Nazis, and in danger even in Amsterdam, she first asked Christopher

Isherwood to marry her so that she could gain the protection of British citizenship. Instead, Isherwood wrote to Auden suggesting that he do so. Auden immediately agreed. She went to England, they were married, and Auden returned to his classroom. The bride and groom had never seen each other before the ceremony and saw each other only intermittently afterward. The bridegroom did, however, quite like his wife in-name-only—he dedicated his 1936 collection of poems to her.

In the spring of 1935, the twenty-eight-year-old poet-playwright-critic-teacher left his school post to take a job with the General Post Office film unit, where he worked on the classic documentary *Night Mail,* a motion picture for which young Benjamin Britten wrote the music. The writer and composer were impressed, each by the other; it was the beginning of a close friendship.

Another documentary film on which both writer and composer worked was *Coal Face,* which was released in 1935, the year before *Night Mail.* In spite of the success of the latter, the muddle of that earlier effort rankled, and it was only being able to work with Britten, to whom he dedicated some poems, that kept him at the job. Soon he decided that he found the work unsatisfactory, and he resigned. A short time later, Britten and he did a documentary film, *The Way to the Sea,* that was a parody of documentary films.[6]

He returned to writing plays: after *The Dance of Death* and the Auden-Isherwood *Dog Beneath the Skin,* another collaborative effort with Isherwood, *The Ascent of F6.* This play, written in Portugal, concerns the weakness of a would-be hero who, in order to overcome neurotic self-doubt, must set out to climb an unscalable summit. As performed, it had incidental music by Britten.

Now Auden was less and less inclined to remain in England. He persuaded his publisher to finance a journey to Iceland so that he could write a travel book. His motive, in large part, was based on a fascination with the place from which he believed his father's family had come. He found the frigid island less congenial than he expected, offering tough food—but good coffee. Yet his visit there, accompanied for part of the time by his friend and fellow poet Louis MacNeice, was productive. He wrote his amusing "Letter to Lord Byron," a largely autobiographical and satirical account of the contemporary world done in the stanzaic form of Byron's *Don Juan.* Its subject was not, essentially, Iceland. And when his *Letters from Iceland,* written in collaboration with MacNeice, appeared, that work was certainly not the conventional travel book that Faber might have expected; its essay-letters and poems include the epistle to Byron, its five sections interspersed with letters addressed to friends, notes on touring the country, an anthology of Icelandic lore, some fictional "letters," and comments on life's travels, on European politics and the rise of Fascism, on the human condition. Wystan Auden could not and would not escape the reality of the larger world.

He was attracted to islands and the idea of islands, not only Iceland but also his native island: His line "Look, stranger, on this island now" provided the titles for his next volume of collected poems, called *Look, Stranger!* in England (1936) and *On This Island* in America (1937). Later, he would spend his summers for a time on the island of Ischia. But Auden could not, finally, live upon an island. His "Islands" from the *Bucolics,* poems of the 1950s, describes such spots as both prisons and places of ego-centered retreat from the mainland. He knew, early and late, that he could never exist in isolation.

By 1936 his poetry was achieving great critical success. It was publicly praised not only by friends like Spender, Day-Lewis, and MacNeice, but as well by prominent reviewers for prominent periodicals. The outstanding exception was F. R. Leavis, who through his influential journal *Scrutiny* attacked him from first to last as a disorganized and self-indulgent or neurotic writer. Auden was puzzled by the attacks, which probably derived from a rather solemnly

moral point of view that could not tolerate the comic, even
flippant, voice often present in even his poetry on very serious matters.

That voice, however, alternated with a lyric quality, as in
the love poems of the 1930s. The most beautiful of these is
"Lay your sleeping head, my love." Like the others, it was
addressed to a young man, but a young man whose identity
the poet would never reveal because he knew it would em-
barrass the person addressed, with whom Auden had had a
brief and intense love affair. In fact, Auden's love poetry is
never specifically homosexual.[7] In spite of Leavis's insistence that he reveled excessively in very personal experiences and memories, his verse on sexual love, on moral
faults and virtues, and on a range of topics that concern
almost everyone was rarely limited by its language to his
own life or the lives of his intimate companions.

His need to take part in the general life was clear. Even
though he was not by temperament a political creature, he
felt impelled by a sense of responsibility to large social and
ethical concerns—impelled to take part now in the Spanish
Civil War. He went to Spain in 1937, intending to drive an
ambulance and so serve the anti-Fascist and Loyalist cause.

In Spain he had an experience that marked the beginning
of a crucial process in his life. He found that all the
churches in Barcelona were closed, and, as he himself was
surprised to discover, he was profoundly shocked. Suddenly
he realized that, having rejected religion for sixteen years,
he had to recognize how the presence of a church was intensely important to him.

Auden's brief function in the war—doing a bit of propaganda but not driving an ambulance or giving medical
aid—was, oddly, given the time and place where he was,
hardly affected by the fact that he was never a Communist
and was indeed a political figure only in the most broadly
humane sense. Yet, in spite of his attempts to act politically,
he continued to feel acutely uncomfortable with the more
extreme activists. He could not forget the closed and ruined

churches or the brutal treatment of the clergy. He was still anti-Fascist, anti-Franco, but he was disillusioned about the totalitarian Left as well. He soon returned to England.

Between 1937 and 1939, the threat of Fascism, and of Hitler in particular, affected all of Britain. Although Auden's leaving his native land late in this period was cause for his being condemned by many, still the matter was more complicated than simply one of personal safety. His career was changing; his devotion to moral principle unchanged.

As he revealed in his poem *Spain,* a poem not didactic enough for some Communist critics, he was consistent in his opposition to Fascist threat. Yet his life was unsettled and in fact uncommitted in other ways. He was attracted to the imaginative Christianity of Charles Williams and thought that Williams embodied "personal sanctity"; even so, he felt unable to emulate the religious novelist. Increasingly, his concern was with people and with close friends in particular: Spender, E. M. Forster, and of course Isherwood, with whom he now again worked at a play, *On the Frontier.* It was a less successful venture than the earlier collaborations. In 1937, John Masefield, the poet laureate, presented to him the King's Gold Medal for Poetry. He was praised by Edwin Muir, Grigson, Graham Greene, Sir Hugh Walpole. He wrote for British radio and edited the *Oxford Book of Light Verse.* But he was not to remain at ease in Great Britain. In more than one sense, he did not yet feel at home. Early in 1938, he and Isherwood left for China.

It seemed difficult in China, as to some extent it had in Spain, to be certain which forces were either just or likely to prevail. There was of course a war going on between the country and the Japanese invader, and Auden's sympathies were certainly with China. But within that nation the rivalry between the Chinese Communists and the Nationalists, like the uncertain alliance between Spanish Communists and the Loyalists, was puzzling.

Leaving the Orient after a few months, Isherwood and Auden sailed to Vancouver and then traveled to New York. There they were made much of, were introduced to sexually available young men and to all the lively and mildly wicked pleasures of this new world. For Auden the New World was just that, a new place and one to which he had to return.

Both men went back to England determined to move to the United States, but Auden was the more determined. In January 1939, they sailed for New York.

They were greeted by Klaus Mann and his sister Erika, still of course legally Auden's wife. They renewed acquaintances and made new friends; through an introduction from Stephen Spender, Auden met Lincoln Kirstein, the Filene department store heir, founder of the New York City Ballet, and patron of the arts, and the two remained friends for life. Yet, to begin with, the new arrival felt himself a stranger. His first poem for the *New Yorker,* published in 1939, reflected on how the houses and tall buildings of the city seemed to offer no place for him and other immigrants or refugees. Auden was admired by young poets and those who cared for poetry; but he had at first no true place in America. Just as he had earlier left one school for another that he preferred only to be homesick for the first, so he now felt exiled from the old home that he knew he had had to leave behind.

He looked for a teaching job and did not find one, although he gave some lectures, on the political state of Europe—but he now wanted to abandon political rhetoric—and on contemporary English literature. At one of these, he was approached by a blond nineteen-year-old Brooklyn College student who wanted to interview him. The young man was Chester Kallman.

Soon Auden was in love with him; and this was at last a total commitment. The relations between older and younger man were not only sexual, or even very often passionately sexual; and for a good part of their lives together they were not sexual at all. Their relationship was personal, intellectual, aesthetic, and enduring.

It was Chester Kallman who introduced Auden to opera, to the gay patois, and, most importantly, to the possibility of loving and being loved without either a sense of transiency or a crippling sense of guilt. In later years, some observers accused the younger man of being callously unfaithful to his mentor, but this relationship was never deeply shaken by the fact of casual sexual affairs on either side with other people; and the bond was not essentially that of taker and giver but was one of like with like. It was mutual, and it lasted until Wystan Auden's death.

Soon Christopher Isherwood moved across the country, going by bus to California where he was to settle—finally, in Santa Monica—in a house looking over a precipice to the Pacific Ocean. Gerald Heard and Aldous Huxley were there already, and a part of California with its center in Santa Monica was becoming almost a British colony.

Auden was, at this point, asked to teach temporarily at St. Mark's School in Massachusetts; the idea of his doing so came from Richard Eberhart, the poet, who was on the school staff. Auden did teach there for just a month and did not care for the school. The boys, he thought, had too much money and too little knowledge. After returning to New York, he set off with his "C," Chester Kallman, for a bus tour of the country, by the southern route to New Mexico—where they met D. H. Lawrence's widow, Frieda. Then they proceeded westward by way of Arizona and Nevada, where the mountains seemed to them fantastic. Auden, still and always a poet of landscape, found in the whole panorama of the American West a physical counterpart of what he had imagined in his verse. At last they arrived in California, and here the scenery of desert, mountain, and sea was even more spectacular.

For a month—it was August—they stayed at Laguna Beach, an unspoiled village then, off major highways and on the Pacific Ocean. Chester Kallman sunbathed, while Wystan Auden wrote. This was a moment in paradise, but only a moment. A world war was imminent, as they both knew.

They returned to New York, which, so much closer to Europe, seemed like the real world. It was there that Auden responded to the German invasion of Poland: In his poem "September 1, 1939," he described himself as sitting in a bar on Fifty-second Street, "uncertain and afraid" and disillusioned about the decade that was ending. The smell of death was in the air. He concluded that people must love each other "or die." What earlier verses including "Petition" had only implied as a possibility was now in process of becoming reality; he was on his journey to a religious conversion.

Just at this time, Benjamin Britten visited the United States, along with the singer Peter Pears, his close companion. They stayed with the Mayers, William and Elizabeth. Dr. Mayer was a psychiatrist, and he and his wife were refugees who had escaped from Nazi Germany to Amityville, on the Nassau-Suffolk border in Long Island. Auden was a frequent visitor there and became especially devoted to Elizabeth Mayer, a charming woman with musical interests. Like many of Auden's close friendships, this one would endure.

Now Britten and Auden worked together on an opera designed, first, to interest schoolchildren, *Paul Bunyan*. Chester had returned to his classes at Brooklyn College, and Wystan was working constantly, writing for long hours in part to distract himself from the bad news that came out of Europe. He also turned again to teaching, at the League of American Writers. But that sort of work, for which he was paid a salary, got him into trouble with the immigration authorities, for he did not have a work visa. After some confusion, some delay, and a special trip to Washington (arranged by Walter and Kate Louchheim), he managed to resolve the problem. He told the authorities that he had not, earlier, been paid to teach, although that was not true. And he was allowed to travel to Canada, to stay a day or so in Montreal and then return simply as a British immigrant. He was still an alien, as yet not an American; he defined his citizenship by saying that he was "a New Yorker."

War was declared in Europe, but nothing happened: there were no battles, no air raids of the sort England was now preparing against. In America, the doctrine of isolationism was widely preached; Europe's troubles were the affair of Europeans. Auden was torn between his own impulse to pacifism and his horror of the Nazis, as well as his continuing sense that no isolation, no safe living on an island, was really possible. To escape the dilemma, he tried not only writing but also physical exercise. However, he was clumsy in exercise classes, and his feet hurt.

In 1939 he went to a movie house in Yorkville, the German area in Manhattan which was, and remained even after America entered the war, a center of Nazi sympathizers; the film was a German version of the Polish invasion, and people in the audience shouted, when Poles were shown on the screen, "Kill them!" If the Communist-forced closing of churches in Spain was a first step in his return to Christianity, this moment was another—he was horrified. He needed an absolute faith to which he could turn for a set of values that explained—with the doctrine of original sin— and condemned, and yet offered hope for the forgiveness of, such attitudes and acts. He needed to define sin and to hope for salvation.

Having already admired the man, he now read seriously the work of Charles Williams, specifically his volume on theology, *The Descent of the Dove*. By Williams he was led to Kierkegaard. Williams wrote that all human beings are related to one another, that each life is sacred, and that one must discern divine purpose in all of history including war, suffering, and grief. Kierkegaard taught that every person must choose between despair and a trust in the divine that reveals individual guilt but surrenders the imperfect self to an unknown divine will which is accepted not through argument but on essentially irrational faith. Auden's own position in "The Prolific and the Devourer" had been one with religious but by no means orthodox implications about a moral imperative that could not be reached by pure reason. Now, in his 1940 "New Year Letter," addressed to Elizabeth Mayer, he argued that one must accept divine law and no other absolute belief, whether political, as in dogmatic Marxism, or psychological, as in Lawrence or the more rigid followers of Freud. The dubious anchors of these absolutes could not sustain themselves on scrutiny, although he thought that Europe was deceived by them and by the false idea of its, Europe's, cultural roots. He decided to remain in America—and, again, he was bitterly blamed by many for not returning to wartime England—because, rootless, skeptical, various and changing and perplexed, this country was a place, even a void, where a thoughtful man could not deceive himself. He had to know that he was alone.

Alone, yes, but alone before God, Kirkegaard would put it. Auden was not often lonely for companionship. He stayed with Erika and Golo Mann in California, seeing Isherwood, too, who was writing movie scripts and studying Vedanta; he visited Lincoln Kirstein's sister Mina Curtiss in Williamsburg, Massachusetts, and gave the Commencement address at Smith College, where she taught English; he was constantly with Chester Kallman. But he now began, alone, to attend church and to say prayers. He had, by the end of 1940, reached the last step in a gradual process of religious conversion. He joined the Episcopal Church. It was a necessary move for him alone, and one that none of his closest and most sympathetic friends took with him.

He had his own very individual views about the Christian religion. The faith, he said, is Catholic, but the process of reaching it may be Protestant. (Anglicans have traditionally declared that their communion is both Catholic and Protestant, that the two are not contradictory terms; but the American Episcopal Church has now stricken "Protestant" from its name, and the word does not appear in the new prayer book. Auden grew away from the Protestant tone.) He thought himself, with his sense of being personally flawed, and not only by his homosexuality, as closer to Augustine, if not Calvin, than to Thomas Aquinas. He believed in prayer, but in a prayer that listens and does not only beg. About such a central doctrine as the Resurrection, he could startle others by admitting that it was perhaps not something reasonable to believe. In church, he gave the responses clearly, and he sang loudly although his voice was less than musical, and he could hardly carry a tune. At first he tried to avoid sermons and homilies, by going to very early service, that is, low mass, when they are generally omitted; but, later he confessed that now and then one heard a good preacher. When possible, he attended a high or Anglo-Catholic church, and at the end of his life he would belong to the parish of St. Mark's in the Bowery, a distinctly high—or, as Auden said, "spiky"—church, where he approved of the priest and his homilies.

Auden's religion did not diminish but rather supported his sense of the comic. Like the Dante of the *Divine Comedy*, he knew that, from the Christian point of view, every fallen human being is silly, flawed, a clown, as well as an infinitely valuable creature. He loved to sing and giggle at hymns that were hilarious in spite of the authors' pious intentions. There was the children's hymn about the saints:

> And one was a doctor, and one was a queen,
> And one was a shepherdess on the green.
> You can meet them in school, or in lanes, or at sea,
> In church, or in trains, or in shops, or at tea.

(He was amused by the idea of "a queen" as holy; and loved the idea of meeting a saint at tea.) And there was the hymn that had the ambiguous phrase, "Peace, perfect

peace, with loved ones far away." Like a good many Anglicans, he saw the endearingly funny aspects of Anglicanism.

Auden moved to Brooklyn Heights late in 1940, renting a
bedroom and front room in a house the other residents of
which included the southern novelist Carson McCullers,
Golo Mann, Britten, Pears, the writers Jane and Paul
Bowles, and for a time the striptease personality (and
writer) Gypsy Rose Lee. He himself took over and insisted
that the others in this extraordinarily disorganized board-
inghouse be punctual for meals. He played the role of
housemother—his timetable was exact even if his clothes
and his bedroom were a mess. He was lecturing now at the
New School for Social Research, and seeing priests and
theologians—Ursula and Reinhold Niebuhr became close
friends—as well as strippers and raffish artists.

The war was now serious and terrifying. For all his attempts to remain in some way detached, he had to declare
his firm commitment to fighting Hitler, even though he was
not yet so outspoken on behalf of American involvement as
the Niebuhrs, Erika Mann, and others who were close to
him. He was aware of being in an awkward position: He
was not an American citizen.

From this point on there were more invitations for him to
lecture, and he performed at the University of Michigan, at
Penn State, and at Yale. His public life in America was beginning to flourish. His private life was a different matter.

In 1941 Chester Kallman took another lover, a young English sailor. Wystan Auden was shattered. Chester was
twenty and looking for new sexual adventure; Wystan was
thirty-four and wanting only to be settled in a relationship
with the one person he had chosen. He had regarded that
relationship as being like a marriage. Chester, grateful, ad-
miring, and yet feeling his to be the subordinate role, had
not. The older man felt momentarily like killing the young
man, the sailor who had seemed to replace him. Then,
alone and grieving, he fled New York, going to Olivet College in Michigan, where Joseph Brewer—who had known

Gertrude Stein, and the literary and artistic world of the twenties and was to be another lifelong friend—served as president. At Olivet, Auden taught a summer session. When he returned to New York, Chester Kallman told him that he wanted their friendship to continue but not as a sexual affair. The two even went together to Rhode Island on a visit. But Auden was not yet reconciled to the situation; and it was a bleak period for him. He wrote a poetic passage about himself as Saint Joseph, believing that Mary was unfaithful to him. And it seemed as though he and his rediscovered faith were being tried as Joseph was tried. While in Rhode Island he learned—Chester told him the news—of his mother's death. He was grief-stricken. Elizabeth Mayer, with her protective love, in part replaced his mother, but nobody could yet replace "Dearest Chester."

In September he went to Ann Arbor as associate professor of English at the University of Michigan. He remained, there, almost desperately lonely. He wrote to Chester, began to worry about Chester's promiscuity as he would, sometimes tearfully, for the next few years, and yet kept busy. Refusing to teach "creative writing," he lectured on European literature from the classics to the nineteenth century, bringing in the opera along with standard poetry and prose. He went to the classroom in jeans and bedroom slippers; and the slippers he would continue to wear on campus from that time on, amusing the students at Michigan and Swarthmore but shocking the more starchy ones at Smith. He made each student memorize long poems and translate, using a bilingual dictionary and their imaginations, from languages that they did not know. And he assuaged his first loneliness by making friends with colleagues, largely married couples with children, for he loved home life. Among his good friends were Albert and Angelyn Stevens (they named their baby, for whom he wrote the poem "Mundus et Infans," after the poet) and the Rettger family. One of his most delightful occasional poems, "Many Happy Returns," was dedicated in 1942 to

John Rettger on his seventh birthday. It may be, however, as
Humphrey Carpenter suggests, that the work was inspired
as much by Chester Kallman's twenty-first birthday.[8] Lacking anything like an immediate family tie now, in a regular
daily way, although his correspondence with father and
brothers was affectionate, he was drawn to families.

In December 1941, with the bombing of Pearl Harbor by
the Japanese, America entered the Second World War. Auden anticipated being called up for military service, but the
university arranged for him to complete the academic year.
Chester Kallman went to Ann Arbor in February, to be a
graduate student at Michigan, and once more he and Wystan Auden lived together, with the young man cooking—
and very well, as Auden said. Although a number of the
poet's friends thought that Chester treated Wystan badly
and indeed they attacked him as a promiscuous opportun-
ist, Auden always defended him (in spite of painful moments) and simply gave up friendships with those who
openly expressed contempt for the young man.[9]

The poet's fantasy of perfect love was shattered. His illusion of peace, and the world's, the "peace in our time" of
Munich and Chamberlain's appeasement of the Nazis
(which Auden deplored), was shattered. But the poet and
teacher continued, for now, to teach his students. He continued to write. And he now produced his finest dramatic
work, *For the Time Being,* a Christmas oratorio about and
for a deeply troubled time.

It was to be set to music by Britten, but it never was. And
so it remained an oratorio only in an oddly poetic sense. It
seemed, as well, to be a very odd way altogether to tell the
Christmas story, for it included slang and bawdy language
along with beautifully elevated lyrics. Ten years later, when
it was presented by a group of young instructors whom Auden befriended at Smith College, and presented at that in a
church—St. John's, the Episcopal Church on the edge of the
Smith Campus—they were nervous as to the likely reaction
from the ladies of the parish. (The ladies loved it.) Auden

himself, with some fear that the modern "low" language of, for instance, the soldier's chorus in "The Massacre of the Innocents" might suggest a blasphemous parody, wrote to his father, who was puzzled, to explain the work's intention. In his letter he observes that his dramatic narrative is not a historical account, but the re-imagining of a religious event that recurs eternally: every December 25 is the birth of Christ *now*. Auden thus makes the biblical shepherds urban proletarians, Herod a modern intellectual, the wise men a scientist, a philosopher, and a liberal humanist, who must give up futile attempts to arrive at absolute truth and instead follow their star. Simeon is a theologian explaining the need for revelation, and the casually brutal soldiers who massacre the innocents are simply mercenaries in the service of a dictator. As Auden comments, the old mystery plays and Italian paintings treated these people and events as contemporary for their audiences and viewers, and he too, instead of picturing biblical persons in nightgowns— and the adult Jesus with "a Parsifal beard"—wants to revive the story using accidental modern persons and places to show that Christ is born anew each year—as now, in 1942.[10]

That summer he spent in Pennsylvania with Caroline Norton and James and Tania Stern. In September, he was rejected for military service not because of problems with his feet, which would probably in any event have kept him out of the army, but on psychological grounds: When asked, he was candid about his homosexuality. Auden had been accused in the British press of wanting to escape wartime duties, but the rejection upset and depressed him.

Having left Michigan for good, while Chester Kallman remained there pursuing graduate studies, Auden now took a position nearer New York, at Swarthmore College, just outside Philadelphia. Although Swarthmore was thought by many academics to be the finest liberal arts college in the United States and he liked his colleagues, he found the students a little dull. They were intelligent enough, but perhaps too soberly serious for him. Originally a Quaker foundation, Swarthmore retained something of the moral dedication of its founders; faculty meetings were less legalistic than in other institutions, with none of the usual nitpicking and professorial windiness, but they had (and still have) very much the quiet unstructured mood of the Quaker meeting, reflective and concerned with consensus rather than motions and votes. Auden did not attend many of them.

At first, then, he was bored at Swarthmore, missed Ann Arbor and Chester—once more, in a new place he longed for the old—and tried to join the merchant marine. Yet he continued busily to write, producing a kind of poetic commentary on Shakespeare's *The Tempest*, called "The Sea and the Mirror."

He could afford to teach only part-time, for he had been awarded a Guggenheim Fellowship for writing poetry. But he did teach conscientiously, and his Swarthmore students found him fascinating if peculiar, often brilliant. He spent the summer with faculty friends in New Hampshire, where he completed "The Sea and the Mirror" with a prose discourse spoken by Shakespeare's inarticulate Caliban in the style of the very articulate Henry James. At the end of his Guggenheim year, in the fall of 1943, he returned to Swarthmore as associate professor. It was true there, as at most American colleges and universities, that even the most celebrated poet achieved the top academic rank much less easily than did a teacher who lacked great scholarly distinction but had a Ph.D. Still, Auden was only thirty-six and felt no reason for complaint. He augmented his modest salary by teaching Chinese naval officers and by taking on an evening course at nearby Bryn Mawr College.

He edited a volume of selections from Tennyson. It was in the introduction to this that he referred to Tennyson as having the best ear of any English poet and being "the stupidest." Some years later he admitted the comment was foolish and that he had of course meant that the Victorian was the least intellectually consistent of the great poets. He revised his earlier poetry for a new collection which Random House agreed to publish, revising sometimes drastically and omitting lines, passages,and whole poems.

In the summer of 1944 he wrote, in New York, what was to be a short poem but one that evolved into the book-length *Age of Anxiety*. In the spring of the following year he was allowed, because of his knowing German and Germany, to take the temporary rank, and wear the uniform of, an American army Major, flying to Europe with a "bombing survey" to discover the results of Allied air attacks upon the continent. He went first to England, where he had not been for almost five years. His tart observations on English weather and food made it clear that he much preferred America in general and New York City in particular.

In Germany, he was horrified by the evidence of death and destruction, by what the Nazis had done to victims in concentration camps but also by what the allies had done, destroying cities and their civilian occupants. The experience shook him too much for him to be able to write—or, very easily, to speak—about it.

Back in the United States, he resolved to support himself by his pen, and he finally gave up regular teaching, although he would continue to lecture and give readings. The Yale University Press made him editor of a Younger Poets series, and he began work for the Viking Press on what would finally be called the *Portable Greek Reader*, an anthology not published until 1948, when it sold so well that it could be said to inaugurate the period of his relative prosperity. This was, indeed, only relative, although he was to say in the early 1950s, when he lived in a Bowery slum flat and wore the most threadbare clothes possible, "For the first time in my life, I'm rich."

His projects were various. He tried a collaborative version of Webster's tragic melodrama *The Duchess of Malfi* with Bertolt Brecht, but the collaborators got on badly and the result was not a success. He gave readings and he ad-

vised younger poets on verse technique. But the most surprising project of this period was his affair with a young
woman, after years of being exclusively and openly homosexual.

She was Rhoda Jaffe, who had been Chester Kallman's
classmate in college. She was separated from her husband,
she greatly admired Auden as a poet, and, like a good many
other women, she found him attractive. (Auden would say
that most women are especially drawn, oddly, to homosexual men.) A serious-minded and quite beautiful woman,
blonde and shapely, she was going through a troubled period and seeing a psychiatrist regularly. Probably Wystan
Auden was attracted to her in large part because she was
precisely not the strong maternal figure represented by most
of his close women friends. She was less mother-like than
daughter-like, a younger woman who needed paternal love.
Fond always of children and families, he regretted not being
a parent. Now a contemporary and friend of Chester's
could perhaps replace Chester not as a beloved and respected son but as a beloved and comforted daughter—and
mistress.

On her part, the affair was understandable for a number
of reasons. She had been reared in an orphanage in Patch-
ogue, Long Island, a major stop on the Long Island railway
for passengers traveling to the island's eastern end, but a
dull town that was neither the city nor the Hamptons; her
once-rich but now bankrupt father virtually abandoned his
children. Wystan Auden was at once a father figure and a
lover. Their love for each other caused negative reactions:
Marianne Moore, a friend of Rhoda, of her husband, Milton Klonsky, and of Wystan, disapproved, whereas Chester,
probably jealous, made wicked fun of the relationship. But
she herself, a gentle young woman without malice, believed
that Auden had been sexually "converted." Although the
change of sexual interest was not to be a lasting one—Auden himself was opposed to homosexuals' marrying and
pretending to be something they were not—he had even

now enough misgivings not to contemplate so serious a bond, a true marriage and not the sort he had, in name only, with Erika Mann. From Bennington College in Vermont, where he was teaching for one term, he wrote to Rhoda that his bed was lonely, adding in his wry and still somewhat "campy" way, "Aren't men BEASTS."

The scoffing Chester, having lost his job, moved in with his former lover and cooked for them both, while the affair with Rhoda went on. Auden seemed to be living now in two worlds. In the summer of 1946 he moved into a ramshackle house that he and the Sterns had bought in Cherry Grove on Fire Island. Of all the Fire Island settlements, Cherry Grove—one of the oldest and one that had always been a raffish center for artists—had got the reputation of having the most overwhelmingly homosexual population. When Chester came to stay, crossing on the ferry from Sayville, he immediately took to the place, and spent his nights in bars and bushes pursuing casual sexual adventures. But Auden loved it, too, as a spot where "nothing is wicked," where one could lounge days away in old clothes or virtually no clothes, sunbathe on a beautiful white sand beach, or stroll along the rickety boardwalks. Spender and Isherwood, with his then lover, visited—and so did Rhoda, to Wystan's delight, only in part because he knew how her presence would surprise and puzzle the regulars at the hotel bar.

In the fall he returned to the city and took a flat in Greenwich Village. It was soon, like any place in which he lived, a filthy shambles. He lectured on Shakespeare at the nearby New School, then—on modern literature—at Barnard College. Finally, in July, *The Age of Anxiety* was published. It was to achieve a large sale and gain the author, in 1948, a Pulitzer prize. It was given public dramatic readings, and a Jerome Robbins ballet was based on the book, using its title. Yet the critical reviews were mixed, a number of them unfavorable.

The affair with Rhoda Jaffe faded, although she and he remained friendly for years, until her death by suicide. At the age of forty, Auden fully recognized his basically homosexual nature and believed that it would mean, for him, a degree of loneliness that would be lifelong. But there was Fire Island, and there were to be intermittent erotic relationships, which involved deep friendship if a fairly subdued kind of love.

If the wild life was not for him, the subject of wild and loose living was one that he could write about. The composer Igor Stravinsky asked him, at the suggestion of Aldous Huxley, to do the libretto for an opera he planned, to be based on the eighteenth-century series of etchings by Hogarth called "The Rake's Progress." Auden, who admired Stravinsky's music, agreed. The work about a deeply divided hero-villain, for Auden's Rakewell is two characters in one, showed the descent of a bold young man into ruin and madness. It ended as a venture undertaken by three rather than two, Chester Kallman working along with Auden on the text for Stravinsky's score. The writers soon discovered that writing opera libretti for the stage and the singing voice was not like writing poems for the page and the speaking voice.

The libretto was completed early in 1948, and Auden and Kallman, collaborators, sailed to England. They stayed only briefly to visit Auden's father, proceeding to Paris—where Christopher Isherwood, who happened to be there, was sprung on Auden as a surprise—and then to Italy. By May they were on the island of Ischia, which they thought one of the most beautiful of all places, and to which they would return for many summers. There, in August, the poet tried his hand at pornographic verse. He may have been motivated by the fact that his was now a chaste life, while Chester Kallman was playing the role of philanderer.

In any event, the poem that he entitled "The Platonic Blow" and intended for Norman Holmes Pearson of Yale (his coeditor for the Viking anthology *Poets of the English*

Language) is of more technical interest as a work of verse than it is effectively erotic. Auden believed that true pornography, by which he said he could be sexually aroused, was essentially nonliterary. This verse is literary and poetically fascinating, but certainly it interests its readers more than it arouses them. The process that preceded its being written suggests in itself a certain detached method. He asked a number of friends, all homosexual, what fantasies most excited them: what would the age, ethnic background, and class or occupation be for the most exciting object of desire, what kind of sexual action would take place, in what setting, and so on. The result describes a "platonic" or ideal encounter with a young garage mechanic who is also the boy next door, half-Polish and half-Irish, in the springtime and in the narrator's own apartment; that encounter involves the slow removal of clothing and oral sexual relations in which the young man is at first quite passive but then affectionate, even demonstrative. The verse includes internal rhyming and a tight metrical pattern. It is in fact all rather formal: no "dirty" words, no shouting, no sadism or anything that could be called kinky. Not a great work of art, it is yet a poet's poem; it seems unlikely that a run-of-the-mill publisher specializing in the hard-core genre would consider it a good financial possibility. It was published, sometimes in a garbled form, without the author's permission, although he had given carelessly typed copies to friends, and he denied authorship, so that he could not claim payment or complain about its appearance. But, once more, his denial, which had to do with his objecting to gross and public displays of sexual acts, or sexual feelings, or indeed passionately religious feelings, was not truthful.

He discovered at last, perhaps after listening to Chester's tales, that on Ischia as in Italy generally a great many young men who are not homosexual are as willing as his Irish-Polish lad to be served sexually. This was to be one, but only one, aspect of his love for the island.

In the autumn he returned to New York to work. Early in 1949, he gave a series of lectures at the University of Virginia on "The Romantic Iconography of the Sea" which was published under the title *The Enchafèd Flood*. It is probably his most brilliant single volume of literary criticism. In the same year he served as one of the thirteen judges for the Bollingen Foundation to decide on the recipient of the first annual Bollingen poetry award. The prize went to Ezra Pound for the *Pisan Cantos,* and the result was shock and controversy, as Pound had clearly been, during the war, both an anti-Semite and a Fascist. Auden defended the award, as he had opposed his own publisher's wanting to exclude Pound from a poetry anthology. It was universally assumed, then, that he had voted for the expatriate poet, then in a mental hospital in Washington. The widespread rumor was that only a few of the judges had cast their votes against Pound. One who announced his opposition was Karl Shapiro. In fact, Auden, like Shapiro, voted against the award. He loathed Pound's politics (although Pound's Fascist rhetoric was something of a pose, and he could be quite apolitical and generous in private). At the same time, he did not believe that either political or moral evils were appropriate causes for denying the genius of a poet; he simply did not think, privately, that Pound, great influence as he was—especially upon Eliot—was a good enough writer to deserve this prize. He gave a different impression publicly. Auden, along with Eliot, Tate, and others, was attacked for his supposed decision to defend and reward a traitor, and he never responded by telling the truth about his vote.[11]

That summer he returned to Ischia, where Chester was already in residence. It was a pleasant time of reading, talking with friends, sunning, and sipping wine. The pattern was now set of his going back to the island summer after summer. In 1949 he also went to Venice for a short time and to Calcutta, where he visited his brother John, the geologist, and met Nehru and his daughter, Indira (later to become Mrs. Gandhi).

Auden divided his time now between New York and Ischia, where he and Chester had a house in the village of Forio, a house with a garden, a dog, and cats. He continued to lecture in America—in 1950, at Mount Holyoke College in Massachusetts—and now and then to visit Spender and other friends in England, where he was in 1951 when Cary Burgess, whom he knew but not intimately, and Donald MacLean defected to the Soviet Union. The two were denounced as spies, but Auden, whom Burgess had apparently wanted to reach and to visit in Italy before or instead of going to Moscow, refused to discuss his friendly acquaintance.

The Auden-Kallman-Stravinsky *Rake's Progress* had its premiere in Venice late in 1951, in the small but distinguished Fenice Theatre, and was a success. The two librettists planned another work, with the idea of Stravinsky's again providing the music; this was *Delia, or A Masque of Night,* but the composer had other projects and never gave it musical form.

Auden's own projects included serving, along with Jacques Barzun and Lionel Trilling, as a judge of books to be included in a book club, the Reader's Subscription. The three got along together, but in literary tastes did not always agree.[12]

Back in New York, Wystan Auden and Chester Kallman moved into a decrepit and dirty apartment in a warehouse on Seventh Avenue. Auden lectured, traveled, wrote, and reviewed, and proposed a second marriage, a "real" one, to an attractive young woman; but nothing came of it. His social life had become very full, with dinners, parties, and the inevitable receptions that went with readings and lectures. When, in 1953 he went, as William Allan Neilson Professor, to Smith College—only seven miles away, and across the Connecticut River, from Mount Holyoke, where he had taught three years earlier—his duties were limited to giving a few lectures and being a presence. But he also took part in the annual Faculty Show, a comic melodrama called "The White Rose of Northampton," which was written and performed by very junior members of the faculty; he sang, in an enthusiastic, if wobbly, treble, the ghost of the heroine's father, to Mozart's music for the ghostly commendatore in *Don Juan*. He also had an affair with an instructor, a young man in his mid-twenties, of whom he wrote in "The Willow Wren and the Stare" as a "white lascivious lamb." He paid the young man a hundred dollars to go through the sixty or seventy poetry typescripts submitted for the Yale series, and to choose the best eight or ten. Leafing through these, Auden asked him which one of the group was the best. He replied, "Daniel Hoffman's." Auden agreed, and it was chosen.

A senior member of the English department, the distinguished critic of American literature Newton Arvin, had fallen in love with the same young man and, while Arvin spent the year as visiting professor at Harvard, had installed the "lamb" in his Northampton apartment. Auden, whose suite in a dormitory was too small for much entertaining, borrowed the apartment for an ambitious champagne party attended by some fifty or sixty people from Smith and Mount Holyoke, from New York and Boston. Most people left by midnight, and Auden went home shortly after that. Chester Kallman and some eight or ten other gay young blades stayed, drinking champagne and rollicking naked or half-naked on the floor and in the sofa bed until morning. Depending on one's point of view, it was the social high point or the social low point of the college year.

The following summer and early fall Auden stayed in Ischia after Chester had left, for October and November, "the loveliest time of all," he wrote, "wonderful clear lights and exciting skies." But he was furious with the "local American Homintern," young men who "have run up debts with all the townspeople which I am perfectly certain they cannot pay." It was, he declared, a "bourgeois fury," but "one can be rich and behave unconventionally; one can be poor and behave conventionally; one cannot be poor *and* behave unconventionally."[13]

Back in America, he decided to move into yet another Manhattan flat, this time on the East Side at 77 St. Mark's Place, just on the Bowery. Some years later, he commented that "nobody" lived in New York anywhere except on the East Side. But his was hardly the so-called smart East Side, for the second-story walk-up flat that he inhabited was as dingy and dirty as the other places in which he had lived. He found it, even so—or perhaps, oddly, for that reason—a congenial place to work and to give parties. His life had now two centers, the flat in St. Mark's Place and the house in Forio, on Ischia. He traveled abroad and gave lecture tours in America, staying overnight, often on college campuses, but the flat and the house were his homes.

When Auden's old friend Cecil Day-Lewis retired as professor of poetry at Oxford, an election had to be held, in which University M.A.'s could vote, to fill the chair. One of the University's most striking and eccentric scholars, Enid Starkie, wrote to suggest that Auden be a candidate. He refused because the post offered so little financial recompense (it involved only being in residence and giving one lecture each term); besides, he was now an American citizen and doubted that he could win election. Enid Starkie, always a strong-minded, independent spirit—she smoked cigars and wore slacks in a setting where women did not do such things—persevered, and he gave in. The other candidates were distinguished writers but not poets, Harold Nicolson and G. Wilson Knight, the Shakespearean scholar (Evelyn Waugh called him "an unknown scholar," but the comment merely displayed Waugh's ignorance). To his own surprise, Auden won the election. He had no idea how he could manage without the dollars in fees he earned from lecturing in the United States, but he did manage.

Even though he was concerned about having enough money to live on, he ventured to write a check for two hun-

dred fifty dollars to help Dorothy Day, the editor of the
Catholic Worker, who operated a haven for the destitute on
the Lower East Side of Manhattan. She had been fined that
amount because the house was judged unsafe under the fire
laws. Auden decided that God would provide for him, as he
helped to provide for others.

As an Oxford professor he was characteristically eccentric and, perhaps uncharacteristically, modest. He had always been inclined to combine pontification in the
classroom with clowning, and now, addressing audiences
from a splendid professorial eminence, he found his position slightly comic. Visited by an American friend, he
ducked with him behind a pillar, pointed at a distin-
guished-looking man strolling casually by, and whispered,
"That's J. I. M. Stewart—Michael Innes, you know!" Almost as much as he had been excited by lunch with Garbo,
he was impressed by his favorite writers of crime thrillers,
even "Michael Innes," whom he had known years before
when he was an undergraduate.

At this point, his life was largely divided between Oxford
and Ischia, although he could soon reduce the amount of
time spent in Britain because the university allowed him to
give his twice annual lectures in a single term—lectures on
a wide range of literary subjects, many of which were collected in his critical volume *The Dyer's Hand.*

Dr. George Auden, the poet's father, died in the spring of
1957, aged eighty-five, and there seemed now even less reason to spend most of his time in England. There was also
less appeal in the idea of remaining on Ischia. Rents and the
cost of buying a house were going up. And a disagreeable
break with his and Chester's houseboy Giocondo involving
money and possibly a three-sided and uneasy sexual relationship—for Giocondo was a handsome young man—
helped to make Auden bid his "good-bye to the Mezzogiorno," to leave Italy and settle in northern Europe.

Wystan Auden and Chester Kallman remained together,
taking a house in Austria, in the small village of Kirchstet-

ten, not far from Vienna. Now Auden's life was to be spent largely there, although each winter he would return to New York.

He traveled in America, but now not very far from the city. He lectured at Princeton; he helped with Noah Greenberg's Pro Musica production of the medieval *Play of Daniel,* for which he wrote some alliterative lines of narration. He went to parties—literary, musical, gay, and serious.

At one such party, in 1959, he met a very tall, blond Columbia undergraduate with pale blue eyes, Orlan Fox. Auden had just completed his prose poem, as it might be called, "Dichtung und Wahrheit," which in its very title revealed his fascination with Goethe, but it was also a work that reflected upon human love, sexual love, more seriously than anything of his had seemed to do for some decades. And at this moment, once again, he fell in love. Orlan Fox was bright and well-read as well as sexually attractive. He soon was serving as Auden's secretary, dinner partner, friend, and, for a time, loved one. They remained close for the rest of Auden's life, and the life of the young man—he died young, in 1987—was virtually devoted first to the presence and then to the memory of the older.

In 1960, Auden published *Homage to Clio,* a volume of verses on the Muse of history, which includes "Dichtung und Wahrheit." It was not enthusiastically reviewed by critics, who wrote that Auden in this later period had lost his freshness and brilliance. The truth is that his interests were now different. He was increasingly concerned with writing for music and writing about both places and ideas either in prose or in what appeared to be prosaic verse. He appeared from now on to be more solemn in his pronouncements and more light and casual, or simply comic, in his poetry. As he commented, he had wanted in his twenties to vex the conventionally middle-aged, and as he approached (and passed) sixty he wanted to upset the conventionally young—including by now most of his fellow poets and critical reviewers.

He and Chester Kallman translated libretti and wrote libretti, including that of Hans Werner Henze's *Elegy for Young Lovers,* which had its premiere in Germany and then, later in 1969, was performed at Glyndebourne. Auden preferred the German production because Dietrich Fischer-Dieskau sang the leading role.

The love affair with Orlan Fox soon cooled into an affectionate relationship, and Auden took up with a Viennese lad, who distressed him by being arrested (in the spring of 1962) for his involvement in burglary, using Auden's Volkswagen. Nevertheless, that affair continued, while Chester Kallman brought Greek boys back to Kirchstetten from his annual holidays. One of these was Yannis Boras, who became devoted to the older poet and drove him on trips to visit friends.

Displaying Auden's interest in and frequent brilliance in articulating critical ideas, *The Dyer's Hand,* that collection of essays which included the Oxford lectures but also other pieces on religion and art, appeared late in 1962. The title comes from Shakespeare's sonnet CXI—"My nature is subdu'd/To what it works in, like the dyer's hand"—and suggests what Keats means in his letter, largely upon Shakespeare's genius, about "negative capability." But a trade journal for the dye industry wrote to the publisher asking for a review copy. Auden loved it and insisted that the copy be sent.

Through Lincoln Kirstein, he met Dag Hammerskjöld of the United Nations. After Hammerskjöld's death in 1961, he was asked to translate a volume of the Swedish statesman's diaries. Auden knew no Swedish, but he had the work literally translated for him to retranslate and edit; it was published as *Markings,* and, although the editor admired the statesman greatly, it included in its introduction a comment on the danger of a great and good man's being tempted to think himself God, a comment that offended the Swedish intellectual and literary community. Auden was advised to strike out the passage if he wanted the Swedish

Academy to award him the Nobel Prize for which, in fact, Hammerskjöld had proposed him. He refused, and he was never given the prize. It was a fact that he regretted, not, he said, because he wanted the honor, but because he wanted the money.

Wystan Auden was hardly the rare instance of a major writer's being overlooked at prize-giving time, and the number of Nobel winners whose names have long since been forgotten is large. But he was reaching the point in his life where money meant more to him. It was not a matter of wanting to live in luxury. He pretended to love the idea of being rich and famous, but his friends could not imagine his dressing, driving, and surviving any way but modestly— not to say squalidly. In fact, before the Oxford professorship which he was afraid would impoverish him, as it did not, he liked to confide to others that he now *was* quite rich from fees for lecturing and reading. He meant that he could eat and drink fairly well, could give something to the church—if he actually had won a Nobel Prize, the money would have bought a new organ for the church in Kirchstetten—and could now and then travel.

In the spring of 1964, he did undertake some traveling. He went for the second time to Iceland, where he visited the spots he had seen some twenty-eight years before with Louis MacNeice. Iceland had changed, for the better, he thought. From there he went on to Sweden, where he visited friends of Dag Hammerskjöld, and at last returned to the house in Austria.

Chester was spending more time in Greece, mostly in Athens, and even gave up living at St. Mark's Place. The flat there was attended to by a cleaning woman, who could not do much to tidy up the mess. The tenant made it clear that the piles of books and papers were not to be disturbed—or the boxes and bottles. Auden experimented a bit with drugs at this point, with LSD and mescaline, but quickly gave them up, deciding that wine was the wiser indulgence. In wine, cocktails, and liqueurs he could and did indulge, with others, a good deal.

He liked his drink: beer at lunch, martinis or gibsons at cocktail time, wine with dinner, cherry brandy or ouzo afterward. Once, when the young man from Smith suggested that they lunch at a Swedish restaurant that served tasty food but, Auden discovered too late, had no beer, he was furious. It was one of the relatively few times when he displayed a bad temper, the others being when a bank check was returned and when he had to wait for someone who was late to an appointment. (He was himself punctual.) As for the alcoholic consumption, it might affect his speech but it did not prevent his speaking—and being articulate, even eloquent. He was not at this point often perceptibly drunk, although stories to that effect have been told. He was arrested once in Berlin and charged with drunken driving, but his erratic handling of the car had more to do with rain, darkness, and his trying to make out street signs—as well as to his being a poor driver—than with any alcohol he had consumed. Asked, in court, if he did drink regularly, he replied that, yes, he did, and had done so every night for all his "adult life." He was excused, and his only comment on the experience, to the music critic Peter Heyworth, was, that the judge had been "rather a dish."

T. S. Eliot died at midwinter, having been ill for some time. Auden had been asked to speak an obituary, which was tape-recorded, and he felt deeply disturbed about doing so, apologizing and explaining to Valerie Eliot, the poet's wife, who was soon to be his widow. The death had special meaning for him: Eliot had been the first established literary figure to read his poetry, had arranged for his first publication by a commercial house, Faber, and had remained an advisor and friend, even though the older poet's own work exerted little influence on that of the younger. Auden spoke of being in a public urinal once with Eliot and being tempted to look down but thinking, "No, it would be like looking at Daddy's."

He did more translating, of poems and opera libretti, still and often working with Chester Kallman. Their work *The Bassarids*, based on the *Bacchae* of Euripides and set to music again by Henze, had its premiere in Salzburg in the summer of 1966. It was a success, not quite so much a success as *The Rake's Progress*, but altogether satisfactory. Certainly, it had come to more than some other tentative projects, including a version of *Don Quixote* that Auden and Kallman had been asked to do and did in fact write, only to have it rejected. The producer wanted not the true rendering of Cervantes' madman but a romanticized version of "the impossible dreams" that came true. (What the producer finally presented was a hopelessly bad distortion, the purely commercial *The Man of La Mancha*, which made money even though, or perhaps because, it was so textually inept and so musically mediocre.)

It appeared that Auden was limiting himself by this time to personal topics. Yet the details of local landscape carried still some greater implications. *About the House*, published in 1965, was written in appreciation of his own modest Kirchstetten domicile. For the poet, however, houses—like cities and countrysides—reverberated with meaning that was social, moral, and psychological or even mythic as well as simply personal.

Auden had always thought of his poetry as being in process. He revised not only handwritten and (badly) typed drafts but the printed lines. When he gave a volume of his to a friend, it was likely to have changes made in pen and ink: words and phrases added, scratched out, or altered. The 1966 *Collected Shorter Poems*, like the 1945 Random House selection and the 1950 Faber first version of collected lyrics, displayed changes in choice of poems and in poetic text. It excluded some poems that are often thought to be of major importance. "Petition" ("Sir, no man's enemy") was dropped because, he said, it ended by commending new styles of architecture, and he liked only old styles. That was a deliberately whimsical comment. He was

friendly with the foremost authority on modern architecture, Henry-Russell Hitchcock, and he did admire some
twentieth-century buildings.[14] "September 1, 1939" was
omitted because he thought it dishonest, but he did not explain how. Other poems were changed, some changed drastically and some virtually rewritten. A good many critics
and reviewers objected to both the exclusions and the re-
writing. Anthony Hecht wrote that he "almost always"
liked the earlier versions better. Auden's response to negative judgments both on his recent poetry and on his altering
of the canon was to tell friends that he was himself the best
judge of his work—and, furthermore, that he now wanted
to avoid the theatrical and memorable sort of verse which
strikes the reader forcefully but fails to tell the truth. He
aimed for a style that would "combine the drab sober
truthfulness of prose with a poetic uniqueness of expression." If he seemed for the moment to be out of fashion, it
might be argued, paradoxically, that by appealing to the
language of Frost and returning to something like the directness of Hardy he was moving decisively beyond the
modern and into the postmodern; and that, in doing so, he
outdistanced his younger critics who, even in the mid-
sixties, were looking backward.

By the time of his sixtieth birthday, in 1967—which he
celebrated in California, with Christopher Isherwood—
Wystan Auden looked far older than he was. His face was
as rumpled as his clothes, deeply seamed like dried and
cracked earth or, as he put it, like a wedding cake left out
in the rain. He had theories about most things, and he had
them on the subject of the physical changes that come with
age. He said, with reference to Falstaff and to himself, that
older men grow stout because the bulk, like baby fat, makes
them seem infantile; what one may wish late in life is just
to revert to being a baby and being taken care of. He did
not articulate theories about what Hannah Arendt called
his "facescape," that countenance that James Merrill (himself well past forty and looking like a sweet-faced adoles-

cent) described as "runneled." It was not so much, in any event, the result of drink and dissipation as it was of neglected and very delicate complexion; his skin was always extremely fair, extremely sensitive. Some of his acquaintances, however, believed that he willed his appearance, wanting to look like an ancient, sagging, and battered monument.

Whatever his own and other people's theories, he took care of others—giving advice, comfort, and money—more than they of him. He disliked grand old men who were ungenerous. And if he deliberately played the vaguely eccentric, vaguely feeble old man, it was his game. He might have lost any intense interest in sex (although he did still frequent call boys) and he might insist on going to bed at nine o'clock, but his writing and his conversation were as vigorous and witty as ever. He was still given to startling the too certain, the smug, unwary audience.

In 1968 the volume of *Collected Longer Poems* was published, and well received. He continued to do translating—putting the old Icelandic Edda into English, aided by Paul Taylor and Peter Salus—and, with Chester, he did an opera libretto of Shakespeare's *Love's Labours Lost* for the composer Nicolas Nabokov. His 1969 volume of poems, *City Without Walls,* won critical acclaim for its spare, direct statement. The title poem of this collection, dwelling in a nighttime mood on the life of the hermit in the orderless city, echoes the poet's earlier lines on the metropolis as place, as society—the city of man, not the City of God—and as the body itself; but here, the stress is upon the speaker's sense that people are hermits, alone in a mechanized "Megalopolis." The poet himself, living in a dingy and dangerous part of New York City, felt lonely.

He asked Orlan Fox to live with him in the Bowery, but that idea came to nothing. More ludicrously, he proposed marriage to Hannah Arendt, who was taken aback by the idea. Afraid of living and perhaps suddenly dying alone, he raised the question of his being allowed to live in an Ox-

ford college, as E. M. Forster lived at Cambridge. Instead,
however, he had to rely on going to visit friends, on traveling out for company. The friends found that, while he was
only in his early sixties, he began to seem crotchety and
old.

The nearest thing to an autobiography that he ever wrote,
as he commented, was *A Certain World,* which appeared in
1970. It was as if he were anticipating his death, to come
three years later.

Still he continued to write, to see new sights, to meet new
people. He visited Jerusalem and, returning to the Ameri-
cas, went to St. Louis and Toronto and then to New Haven.

There, at Yale, he conferred with a young faculty member, Edward Mendelson, whom he had briefly met before,
who had written his Ph.D. dissertation on Auden's poetry,
and whom he now asked to gather and edit his essays and
finally, to serve as his literary executor. (His earlier choices
had been the poet William Meredith, who taught at Connecticut College, and the editor of *The Sewanee Review,*
Monroe Spears, author of a valuable critical study on Auden's verse.)

One of the points Auden insisted on was that his acquaintances be instructed to destroy all the letters he had
written to them. It was a demand which virtually no one
heeded. The drafts of early and published poems, handwritten in ledgers that the poet often gave to friends, were also,
whatever his wishes, to be saved. There are such ledgers in
the Berg Collection of the New York Public Library, in the
Widener Library at Harvard, at Swarthmore College, and
in private collections, although even yet, and even for Edward Mendelson and Barry Bloomfield, Auden's bibliogra-
phers, there is uncertainty about the whereabouts of all this
material; unfortunately, a valuable ledger given to Orlan
Fox was stolen.

For some years, Auden had been amusing himself and
friends by writing clerihews, short comic bits of verse that
rhyme *aabb* and are otherwise free in form, varying in

length of line. They can, in fact—or Auden's could—be yet more free and have a fifth line added, so as to rhyme *aabbb*. Some of these, on a number of literary and historic persons, were published in the 1955 *Homage to Clio* under the heading "Academic Graffiti," and in 1971 he collected a number, to publish them under the same title as a separate volume. Critics were inclined to find such exercises trivial, but, again, the poet refused to draw a line between art and joke.

In February 1972, he celebrated his sixty-fifth birthday, and he bid farewell to New York. He was to return only briefly, to do a final packing and moving.

His *Epistle to a Godson* (the godson was Philip Spender) received good critical notices. Arrangements had at last been made for him to live in Christ Church, his college at Oxford, and he spent the winter there. The residence there was his "grace and favour" cottage, that is, a home provided without rent by dispensation of, usually, the Crown, but in this instance, the university. He celebrated his return at last to English living and English weather by writing the poem "Thank You, Fog." In all, he was glad to be where he was; always the poet of specific times and places, of the calendar, the map, the house plan, he still celebrated the locality as well as its weather. Yet, he felt tired as well as retired. He seemed to his friends prematurely old. And his consumption of alcohol increased alarmingly.

When the Auden-Kallman-Nabokov *Love's Labours Lost* was first performed, he went to Brussels for the premiere. And in April he returned to Kirchstetten. There he wrote "A Thanksgiving," and his health and spirits appeared to improve. He planned new editions and made, even now, revisions of his work. But he was, all the time contemplating death. In the libretto that he and Chester Kallman provided for composer John Gardiner's *Entertainment of the Senses,* he wrote of the need to enjoy life, as there was no sex "in the grave" (he was echoing Andrew Marvell's lines, "The grave's a fine and private place/ But none, I think, do there embrace.") and then in what was probably the last verse he composed, he said of himself that, while loving life, he yet hoped that the "good Lord would take him." He died of a heart attack, in the Kirchstetten house, on September 28, 1973.

His funeral was held in the village, with the local Roman Catholic priest and an Anglican priest officiating together. Beforehand, there was a recording played of Siegfried's Funeral March, the grand music by Wagner that Wystan Auden had said he wished to have played "when my time is up." Not all his wishes could be honored, however. He had also said that when he died he would like his friends to roast and eat his body, as a feast which would be both a cannibal rite (like Montaigne, he respected the mores of cannibals), and a version of the Communion; it would also symbolize his becoming a part of his dear ones, and the idea might even echo his lines on the death of Yeats, "The words of a dead man/ Are modified in the guts of the living." His body was buried in Austria; his words and his presence were recalled shortly afterward in a memorial at the Cathedral Church of St. John the Divine in New York City, with that edifice full of his friends and readers; and his achievement was honored a year later in London, at Westminster Abbey, where John Betjeman, the poet laureate and Auden's friend since college days, dedicated a stone inscribed with his name in the Poet's Corner. There he is symbolically present along with Chaucer, Shakespeare, Milton, Wordsworth, Keats, and Tennyson.

Chester Kallman, the sole heir, died within a year, leaving a legal tangle about manuscripts left either at or to— and the courts decided it was "to"—the Berg Collection of the New York Public Library. Dr. Kallman, Chester's father, had married Dorothy Farnan, who had been his intimate companion for years, and they both maintained inheritance rights, although they were finally granted only royalties. Dorothy Farnan had been close to both Wystan Auden and Chester, but especially to Chester; one evening, in a lighthearted moment, she had persuaded them that they should all plaster their faces with cold cream, and there was a good deal of merriment about the result. Some years after both had died, she wrote an account of their relationship, one essentially sympathetic, but with enough detail to inspire from reviewers some caustic remarks about the younger man's behavior. Auden if alive, would have defended Chester, as always.

The last book of Auden's verse, published posthumously in 1974, took its title from the 1972 Oxford poem—it was *Thank You, Fog.* In the same year, Stephen Spender put together a volume of short pieces, *W. H. Auden: A Tribute,* with comments and anecdotes by thirty-five friends, colleagues, and admirers. Since then, a number of memoirs, critical studies, and biographies have appeared. It seems likely in the last decade or so of the twentieth century that the reputation of Wystan Hugh Auden as one of the century's greatest writers will stand firm.

2

Poetry

W. H. Auden's earliest poems, written between the ages of sixteen and twenty, exist mostly in manuscript. They display unusual skill, a formal control that is rare in adolescent verse. His lines echo the poetry of Hardy and other late Victorian and modern writers, but they are more than imitations. They introduce Auden's personal and continuing interests in landscape, mines, and machines, as well as times of day and times of life. "Landscape," "The Old Lead-Mine," "The Old Colliery." "Sunday Morning." "Easter Monday." "Winter Afternoon." "Daily Bread": The titles evoke those topics and themes. The young poet was, during his Oxford years, exploring possibilities and at the same time breaking away from conventions, including not only standard kinds of meter and rhyme but also, after a time, the conventions of such an unconventional poet as Gerard Manley Hopkins.

In Auden's first published collection of poetry, the one privately published by Stephen Spender in 1928, the Oxford student's untitled pieces reveal elements of an emerging style, but evidences of uncertainty and hesitation too. One element is ellipsis, the omitting of articles and other connecting words, to produce a terse and choppy rhythm. The practice may owe something to Hopkins, but the effect is different, not what Hopkins called "sprung rhythm," but something more staccato. Another element is the use of imperfect or "slant" rhymes. Again, Auden's practice was probably affected by that of an earlier poet, Emily Dickinson, but his rhyming is even more playful and more insistent than hers. In one passage of couplets, he rhymes *country* with *content, fell* with *call, yesterday* with *valley, study* with *quarry, swallow* with *willow,* and *copse* with *corpse.*

Landscape and love are recurrent and related subjects in the 1928 poems: Landscapes may have treacherous passes and uncertain borders, as love may betray one. A haunting line from this untitled verse suggests the promise, doubt, and sense of danger that fill this untitled verse: "Some say the handsome raider, still at large,/ A terror to the Marches, in truth is love."

In his early twenties the poet becomes more cryptic, more uncertain—even his handwriting falters and turns into illegible scrawl—and more difficult. A great deal of what he wrote throughout the early years, he chose not to publish. Yet much of this poetry can tease our curiosity and seem too fascinating to ignore. When, after Oxford, he spent a year in Berlin, he filled a sizeable ledger with first drafts of poems some of which were later printed in revised form; others he appears to have rejected. One of the poems that saw print, and which has been thought of as an important lyric by most critics, was that verse that he later entitled "Petition." This begins with an address to God, "Sir, no man's enemy," which echoes both Herbert's and Hopkins's use of "Sir" rather than "Lord" in prayers. Although written in 1929, it was dated "1930" for the Faber volume published in that year. The prayer-poem asks forgiveness for ills spiritual, sexual, moral, and aesthetic. The "neural itch" of lust, the "coward's stance." It is concerned with the direct relation between moral and physical illness. reflecting the ideas of Layard in the phrase "liar's quinsy"; and it endorses psychiatric "healers" along with "new styles of architecture" and "a change of heart."

Never printed, a long passage in the manuscript draft of this poem, one that constitutes the middle part, begins elliptically and in mid-line,

> are everywhere
> In desert as the hot extravagant glare
> As flash on hills, warning of physical death,
> Upon all surfaces, above, beneath,
> At all times several yet always one
> A gymnast's rhythm at Athens, or then
> A celibate and certain faith at Tintern.[1]

The rejected passage goes on to cite and echo other writers as well as Wordsworth (whose "Tintern Abbey" is referred to here). Perhaps the Greek gymnast and the Romantic poet seemed to enlarge the poet's cast of characters too much, for it already includes, in this poem, faint allusions to Freud, possibly Jung, probably Frank Lloyd Wright, with overtones of D. H. Lawrence, John Layard, Karl Marx, and with Hopkins in the wings. The most striking fact about the poem, still, is its form as a prayer: It appears to predict the later reconversion of the poet to his childhood religion. Yet, later, he may have felt that it was a too forced or not wholly sincere treatment of a serious matter.

Possibly the most interesting complete and completely unpublished poem in the manuscript of 1929–1930 is one that begins "Words Cannot Stop." It reveals Auden dwelling upon his own concern with and frustration about forming a true poetic language. The poet's words, apparently of love, seem yet inadequate and die away, dissolving in "the faithless air."

The *Poems* of 1930, published by Faber and Faber, marks the poet's first appearance to a general public; it includes, along with the final prayer, a series of verses on love and youthful sorrow, and it develops in a number of lines the geography of emotions that was Auden's special territory. Watershed and border, "Sentries against inner and outer," the need for "Control of the passes": all this phrasing carries a sense of someone in transition and uncertainty. Among the more often reprinted poems, the one that begins "It was Easter as I walked out in the public gardens" contains a characteristic mixture of seasonal and religious reference with personal doubt, fear, and anticipation. Its second section begins with lines that might be taken to summarize the mood of Auden and of Auden's poetry at this point, "Coming out of me living is always thinking,/ Thinking changing and changing living."[2]

The poet was changing and absorbing influences, forming his own style, a telegraphic style—as Louis MacNeice commented in a favorable review of the 1930 volume (which left *Times* and *Listener* reviewers baffled)—while he echoed other and earlier styles. His combining of apparently disparate elements may have been what led some early readers to think him difficult and obscure, although obscurity was above all what he wanted to avoid. Another 1930 poem, not included in the Faber volume but written for a play, the manuscript of which was lost, is that beginning, "Doom is dark and deeper than any sea-dingle." Entitled "The Wanderer," it is an imitation of Anglo-Saxon verse in both its subject and its alliterative form. For an audience unacquainted with Old English and unaccustomed to telegraphic terseness, such poetry could only be mysterious. Yet Auden remained steadfast in his determination to be a public, readable, and not a private or affectedly "modern" writer. His 1936 "Letter to Lord Byron," that poem which he wrote while he was visiting Iceland, is a straightforward imitation of Byron's *Don Juan,* done in the stanza and canto form of that satiric work, and filled with witty comments on the oddities and follies, the people and the institutions, of England as well as of the land in which he was composing it. There are critical glances at writers past and present, including I. A. Richards, T. S. Elliot, Roy Campbell, as well as Milton, Bunyan, Pope, and the poet for whom the young Auden and the young Byron shared some crotchety distaste, Wordsworth.

One lyric from the mid-thirties that shows his desire to celebrate the ordinariness of familiar kinds of people is "Who's Who," which makes plain how the great and celebrated persons of the world share commonplace experiences with all the others. The great man in this charming poem had struggled up from an obscure, unhappy childhood to his fame; he was in love with someone who did little jobs around the house, read the celebrity's letters casually if at all, and kept none of them.

Auden's fascination with time and place is everywhere apparent in his early poetry, as in the 1935 lines upon England, "Look, stranger, on this island now"; and his feeling of time and place is often haunted by the knowledge of mortality and danger. He was very much aware of Hitler's rising to power in the Germany where he had briefly lived, and of the vulnerability of "this island," Britain. He was aware, too, of how vulnerable simple people everywhere could be, those trusting in civilized life and in romantic love. "As I Walked Out One Evening," a poem of 1937, touches upon the disillusionment of men and women who believe in promises of justice and fidelity: After all extravagant protestations, they "look into the mirror" with distress. Time takes away their hopes, and finally the clocks stop chiming; but that "deep river" which is time's very image still runs on. Places and times are, in the lyrics of these years, uncertain, tentative—whether the season is summer or autumn, the setting a garden or "Oxford" or "Dover."

Still, if much of this poetry is poignant, it is never sadly sentimental. Auden's combination of tough language, responding to the hard facts of life, and of genuine pain for human suffering is no better represented than in his ballad called "Miss Gee," a grim lyric of 1937. The maiden lady in that poem squints, has narrow sloping shoulders, and lives in a poor "bed-sitting room," where she knits things for the church bazaar and dreams of love and luxury. She is plain, she is pious, she prays—and she is dying of cancer. Apparently she suffers from what Auden elsewhere calls "ingrown virginity." The flatness of the language in this deliberately singsong verse underlines all that is bleak and undignified about the most ordinary everyday pain. Like so many of Auden's pieces, this is a distinctly "unpoetic" piece of poetry: He will not offer the comfort of tragic grandeur.

A counterpart to that poem, in a way, is yet another written in the same year, "Victor." The title is ironic because the man whose shabby story it tells is no victor any more than Edith Gee is, Or "James Honeyman"—in a third poem of this period, about a chemist who devises a poison gas that destroys him. Victor lives a life of frustration, marries an unloving wife, grows to resent her coldness, and at last kills her. He ends his pathetic life in a madhouse. 1937 was, in all, a hard year for Auden, or at least for the creatures of his poetic imagination.

Grimmer times yet, for Wystan Auden, for Great Britain, and for the world, were soon to come. He had again and again to face in honest poetry the reality of betrayal, random pain, and death. One of his best-known poems from this period, "Musée des Beaux Arts"—written in 1938—suggests that art itself, the beauty and the power of mimesis or of a true observation, must represent disasters. The poem has to do with painting, specifically with Brueghel's picture of "Icarus," in which the overambitious figure who has tried to fly with manmade wings falls into the sea to drown, while the figures in the foreground ignore his death. Just so, dogs and horses go about their "innocent" animal lives while the miraculous Christmas birth occurs—and while a saint is brutally martyred. The Old Masters, say these lines, knew that life goes on its way quite regardless of horrendous events.

In the middle and late thirties, Auden became interested in art and artists, in painters and musicians as well as poets. He wrote on "The Novelist," and on "The Composer," as well as on such specific figures as "Rimbaud," "A. E. Housman," and "Edward Lear."

In many of these poems, a reflection can be seen of the poet's sense of himself as an artist—and of his own art. When he wrote about Voltaire living in a Europe of nighttime horror and having to "go on working," he was certainly reflecting on his own world in 1939, a place and time of darkness, of terror, and on his own need to work. Several of these pieces upon writers bring in characteristic imagery as well as current responses to this time and place: "Matthew Arnold" describes the poet and critic who denounced an "optimistic generation," just as Auden could now denounce his own thirties generation, as a "dark disordered city"; and this language is echoed in the best-known of the poems on dead poets, the great elegy for Yeats.

That piece is in part a fiction; it emphasizes the cold weather and frozen waters, although in fact Yeats died in the south of France, which was fairly warm, and it pays tribute to a man whom Auden personally disliked. Like so many poetic tributes of the kind, including Milton's "Lycidas," it is at least as much about the poet himself and his sense of vocation as it is about the person being memorialized. The poem uses Auden's familiar metaphors of place. Yeats becomes a city, with squares and suburbs that are silent as the man himself slowly dies. The beautiful final section begins, "Earth, receive an honored guest."[3] The last short and solemn lines, hypermetrical trimeters, reflect upon language and the lyric poet's duty to his words, to his world: He is to make "a vineyard" of that fallen world and, finally, "teach the free man how to praise." This is an attesting of Auden's conviction that poetry is celebration.

Auden's rejecting of his own generation and in a sense of his immediate past is made clear in "September 1, 1939," a poem that he came later to regret and to reject as an exaggeration. The verse itself, set in a bar on Fifty-second Street in Manhattan, begins with a comment on the whole decade of the 1930s as a "dishonest" time; already, the poet is concerned with the necessity to be honest in what one says and does, just as, later, he was to prefer poetic honesty to poetic display.

A series of verses that had been mostly written somewhat earlier but were not published until March 1939, when they were in part incorporated into the Auden-Isherwood *Journey to a War,* was originally entitled just "In Time of War." This is a sonnet sequence, with a long "verse commentary," that is about the war in China—but much more. The first sonnet (after a dedicatory one to E. M. Forster) is a fanciful reworking of the Creation in Genesis, and the succeeding sonnets give an account of Adam and Eve, their fall and expulsion from Eden. It soon becomes apparent that in an oblique way the sequence has to do with the development of the self, the human self with all its egoism, evil, and promise, which is also the poet's own self, growing, changing, twisting and being twisted through varying weather and landscape. Yet this is no version of Wordsworth's *Prelude,* for the climax comes not as the full development of the poet's mind but rather as a wandering among mountains, a sense of the imperfect, uncompleted life in an alien place, literally in wartime China. There is something fragmentary, something unsatisfying about the sequence— the commentary is verbose and perhaps obscures more than it explains—but it includes brilliant passages and seasonal as well as topographical images that work well. It includes, too, some memorable lines, including the penultimate one in the last sonnet (XXVII), "We live in freedom by necessity."

The 1940 *New Year Letter,* addressed to Elizabeth Mayer, reads as an extended, imaginative speech, serious and yet not ponderously formal, in iambic tetrameter couplets and thus rather tight but at the same time free in its verbal movement. It is about the world at war, a world in "spiritual disorder," and about the task of art which is to "set in order"; yet it recognizes that words cannot stop war. While attesting to the influence of earlier poets, from Blake to Baudelaire, Rimbaud to Rilke, this lengthy poem in three parts is in effect a spoken letter, personal in many of its allusions, general in its discourse upon the end of one decade and the beginning of another. It was published in a 1941 volume entitled *New Year Letter* in England, and, in

America, *The Double Man*. The latter title is from Montaigne by way of Charles Williams, whose *Descent of the Dove* was a major influence on Auden; but it reflects as well the importance for him of the existential Kierkegaard, with his idea that every person has two natures by virtue of the two relationships with God, that of the spirit—if one has faith—and that of the body. The spirit must be embodied, incarnate, and so there can be no absolute division in this twofold nature.

Included in the 1940 volume is "The Quest," a sonnet sequence that is largely, but freely, Freudian, having to do with conscious anticipation and largely unconscious memory. Of the series Auden said that the traditional quest, for the Grail, for adventure, for the Father, for *con*quest, was here meant to be equally "objective and subjective"; again, the self is both the human self and "I myself." The images evoked in these poems are characteristic: the door to future and past in the first sonnet and, in the second, the watch as instrument giving order to time but, like every instrument and measure, providing no answer to the human situation. The succeeding poems picture a familiar landscape of badlands and crossroads, unfound castles and broken bridges, village and city, the park, the library, a "ruined corridor," the tower of the magically talented. These are the various locations in the quest for self-awareness, a quest that without maps—which often self-deceiving beings lack—is still endless, still uncompleted. Section XIV, on "the Way," with an overtone of oriental mysticism but also perhaps echoing "the Way of the Cross," varies the sonnet form. While it contains the standard number of lines, fourteen, it is composed in long, metrically irregular couplets. This odd insert represents a point of balance and a climax. It suggests at least the possibility that one finds the true self by being "not" oneself. The whole sequence concludes in XX with a sense more religious than psychological that the quest or journey of life has as its goal a primal innocence, a selfless love, an Eden rediscovered.

How was Eden to be described? For the poet, that question meant asking, "Where do you want to live, ideally? Where would you be most at home?" It was a question he asked friends, in a sort of questionnaire-game. His own answer was, he said, that he wanted to be in a pleasant house within a great green park, but in the center of a city. There he could play croquet, his favorite game, observe unspoiled nature, and yet have access to libraries, parties, and the opera.

He wrote repeatedly of landscape and location, giving psychological, moral, and finally religious meaning to spots on the map—his 1933 "Paysage Moralisé" had made the first intentions clear—so that (as in Arnold and Tennyson) islands literally signify isolation, escape, and self-absorption, while cities are, again literally, the centers of civilization, mountains are where one achieves eminence and power at the risk of losing connection with the quiet and innocent, if also ignorant, valleys and plains.

The poems of the period 1939–1941 are filled with particulars of place and time that can be transformed into abstract and sometimes puzzling ideas. In Auden's time-space continuum there is both definiteness and mystery; and there is always a sense of celebrating the spot, the occasion. What is often dismissed in the work of other poets as amusing "occasional verse" becomes for him crucially important, whether he is writing of a marriage as in his lines entitled "In Sickness and in Health" (for Maurice and Gwen Mandelbaum) or of a "Blessed Event" or of a birthday—the birthday, in "Many Happy Returns," of seven-year-old John Rettger. The birthday poem is both one of the most delightful and one of the most significant poetic statements of the early forties (it is dated February 1942): It reflects on how all people play roles, like actors, how they must accept their true roles and reject other possibilities, how they must "love without desiring" what they are not. It represents what may be called Auden's specific genius for balancing lighthearted tone with moral message, sensual vitality with intellectual firmness. Its last line is a commonsensical bit of advice: "Follow your own nose."

The lyrics Auden produced in the mid-forties are both observations on real people in real places and attempts to achieve a spiritual order, an honest order, which was the goal of his own quest. His 1940 return to Christianity had been an intellectual decision. Now he was concerned with immediate and practical implications, with how a commitment to faith should affect friendship, love, behavior. His 1942 "Canzone" ends, "There must be sorrow if there can be love," and in his more personal verse there is both. But if he displays something of the inner life in this work, he is at the same time commenting on the sorrows and loves, the interests and needs, of others, of the small child in "Mundus et Infans," of the mysteriously happy woman "In Schrafft's," of "all my friends/ And these United States" in "A Walk After Dark." As the last phrase in that poem may indicate, he was taking on the role of public poet as well. He wrote Phi Beta Kappa poems for Harvard in 1946, "Under Which Lyre" (a lengthy piece that ends in abbreviated decalogue: "Thou shalt not" obey the dean, answer questionnaires on politics, be friendly with advertising men, or "live within thy means"); and for Columbia in 1947, "Music Is International."[4]

Music and drama continued to attract him; he was now at work on his Christmas Oratorio, while he continued to contribute lyrics to periodicals, including the *New Yorker*. His projects and his contributions were by now so numerous that he lost track of some—as he lost track of printed versions.

He was, the poems show, becoming aware of where he was going and where he had been; he retained and developed a constant, yet constantly varied, set of themes: seasons and, again, spots, the physical, the psychological and moral geology, geography, history of both the world and the mind. "In Praise of Limestone," a poem of 1948, gives both personal and general expression to a sense of how important stonescape can be. Limestone, because of its adaptable nature—it "dissolves in water"—becomes a delightful and a mothering formation, an appropriate background for the younger son who can, perceiving its malleable charm and imagining his own possibilities, shape it by charm and teasing and get thereby "more attention than his brothers." Wystan Auden was the youngest of three brothers, and he is writing about family life—but also about his becoming a poet. The limestone lad may be tempted to leave the valley of his environment, tempted by the hard granite wastes which represent political power or the gravel of the plains on which armies can be marshaled, or the great ocean of free, irresponsible adventure. But he returns, as the poem finally returns, to that valley of limestone with its underground streams, where it is possible to believe in true love and a future life.

There are other lyrics upon places and travel: "Ischia," about the Italian island that was for some years the poet's summer home, "An Island Cemetery," and "Not in Baedeker," a poem on the subject of (in Blake's words) the mental traveler. The most complete and richest group of poems on geographical location, its weather and its fully imagined significance, is the series entitled *Bucolics*. Elsewhere, cities figure importantly in Auden's verse. Here he concentrates upon the countryside.

Each of the poems in the series is dedicated to a friend; these include Nicolas Nabokov, the British scholar Isaiah Berlin, and the critic Elizabeth Drew, also British by birth but a professor of English at Smith, where Auden had come to know her well. There are seven bucolics in all, "Winds," "Woods," "Mountains," "Lakes," "Islands," "Plains," and "Streams."

"Winds" is in fact about both wind and weather, both divine inspiration—a kind of wind or breathing—and constant change, the uncertain weather of human life. The language is odd and often playful; the Creator, at the beginning, is "our First Dad," and his human creature is originally good—because he is loved—but "bubble-brained." Perhaps, these lines reflect, the Fall and death would never have occurred if God had chosen to inspire a fish or insect instead of humankind. Still, wind, whether creative or destructive, makes our weather in this fallen world, and the speaker cannot imagine a true city in which people do not talk of weather and look at the rain gauge. The third and final section of this lyric is about the poet and classical inspiration, that of Athena as she is perceived to be the source of wind as well as wisdom, inspirer of poets as well as heroes. In these lines she inspires *anamnesis,* recollection, and the use of that elaborate term makes a neat contrast to the simple final evoking of what is recollected, ordinary scenery and "a few dear names.

Underlying this and the succeeding nature poems are ideas moral and religious. The inspiriting wind in these lightly wavering lines suggests the inbreathing of the Holy Spirit. In the next poem, "Woods," the poet's subject is treated with formality—regular iambic pentameter rhyming *ababcc* ("Winds" lacks terminal rhymes), with unusually literary rhetoric that echoes the Augustans and Milton before reverting to a kind of slang. There is a sense of needing to control and civilize, in the order of verse, the disorder of nature. Geologically, biblically, and poetically, the poems in sequence make up a historical evolution. The water of seas and oceans is deliberately omitted from that sequence; otherwise the physical progression is loosely one of terrestrial development: out of a blazing whirlwind, water and land, then vegetation or primitive forests, the upheaval of mountains and the evolving of lakes, movements of land masses and the phenomenon of islands either fragmented or volcanic, the appearance of arid plains and fertilizing rivers. The beginning of such a movement is found in Genesis, where there is first a mighty wind and then the creation of growth, of fruit and trees; and, according to long tradition, mountains arise on earth only after the Fall and expulsion

from Eden, to be followed by other irregularities upon the
originally perfect earth's smooth surface. "Woods," then,
goes from creation and inspiration to a sense of original
wildness and of the need for ordering, trimming—for civilization. Rustic woods are places of savagery but a "well-
kempt forest" appeals to the grace and favor of, not now
the Creator or the Greek Goddess but the Virgin. "Our
Lady" combines the Hebrew and Christian sense of gra-
cious inspiration with the pagan sense of poetic inspiration.
Finally, this poem concerns culture, agriculture of a sort
that represents all human culture. True culture is displayed
by cultivated woods. Although this is the most bucolic, perhaps, of these *Bucolics*, it introduces the formal note, the
need for civilizing, reminding one not only of Auden's ideal
place to live—a wooded park within a city—but also of his
means to characterize nations by describing the parks in
their great cities: Paris, with its excessively pruned, formal,
grassless parks; London, with its verdant but very largely
tamed Hyde Park; New York, with its seemingly wild and
irregular Central Park, which actually is well-ordered to
create a countryside of ebullient nature within a city of steel
and glass.

The poetic evolution in this series may be more subtle
than the physical and geological, the biblical and mythic. It
involves a shift in person that occurs in the next four poems: here, "I" enters in—indeed, obtrudes, now and then
with perverse petulance—so that, while the first person has
been incidental in the verses on original wind and primitive
woods, that word now is central. We proceed from world-
awareness to self-consciousness, but we are moving toward
the completely social, which means something more than
the neatly civilized. "Mountains" begins, "I know a retired
dentist" (probably Chester Kallman's father in reality), and
goes on to describe mountains as walls, places of dour isolation, if also of safety, where cats may live in comfort but a
"creature who has gone wrong," a human being and more
specifically the speaking self, cannot long live. The poet's

distaste for the cold heights of genius that in its prime egoism cuts itself off from the commonality of people must
surely be embodied here.

The pattern of the series is not, however, schematically
perfect. There is variation from fairly tight to fairly loose;
"Mountains" has an odd terminal rhyme scheme, *abcdef-
ghih*, and the next poem, "Lakes," has none at all. Here,
egoism is not cold but domesticated, merely self-indulgent.
The speaker is comfortable with small (but not great) lakes;
and the poem concludes comfortably and playfully in lines,
saying "I" am not likely to keep a swan or build a tower on
a little rise. The last stanza has been regarded as too offhand, even trivial, suggesting a poet in his dotage: Just
hearing the names of various kinds of lakes is "ever so
comfy." The point is that these bucolic lines have gone from
the cosmic to the almost comic, from primitive force and
form to private comfort. The movement is deliberate, not a
reflection of a poet's changing, for "Winds" was written
after all the others.

Nor is the private voice exclusive. "Islands," a tightly dis-
ciplined poem that rhymes *abcb* and alternates iambic tetrameter with iambic trimeter lines, observes sardonically
how pleasant it seems to be "Me" alone, but it rejects the
isolated life, island existence, once more. The poet in his
poetry must tolerate others and live on the mainland.

That does not mean, however, having to live on "Plains";
in the poem so entitled there is fear of the flatland on
which all seem not just equal but the same, where the self is
exposed without hope of oddity or adventure, of rising to
heights at all or spending some time of retreat upon an island—perhaps Fire Island or Ischia. The vision of a perfectly flat landscape is a nightmare vision. These lines end
cryptically with the reminder that nothing is perfectly beautiful even in poetry, "which is not the case." That is, poetry
can after all be lovely only by honestly displaying real un-
loveliness. The implication seems to be that all plain per-

sons are plainspeople, as they know in their worst dreams,
and yet can imaginatively retreat to various landscapes of
the mind, parks, heights, and rivers.[5]

And, after all, there can be rivers even on the plains. The
final bucolic poem of the series is "Streams," and just as
the end of the "Quest" was innocence, this ending evokes
pure and innocent water, the element that purifies as it bap-
tizes. Now Auden's freely flowing lines are personal, with
the memory of dozing and dreaming in Yorkshire, but they
are finally communal: The final wish is to run as streams
run—the ideas of individual history and social history as
flowing constantly in time are involved here—and this is to
"run with the human race."

General human sympathy and special human love are
central to the shorter lyrics of Auden in mid-career. These
can suggest a lightly humorous feeling about oneself as
lover of the race and simply as lover. The verses collected
under the title "Five Songs" have to do mostly with sorts of
love, and one of them, first entitled "The Willow-Wren and
the Stare," is about erotic love and its larger implications.
In it, two birds, the starling and the wren, overhear and
discuss a human love scene. The wooer addresses his beloved as a "duck" and "lascivious lamb," asking forgiveness for his own greed and clownishness. This is vintage
Auden. When the couple embrace, the wren asks if it is
"only that," and the starling answers, "It's that as well":
Love is sexual and sensual, and yet more. When at last the
wren asks if the lover even knew what he meant, the other
bird's answer is *"God only knows."* The response is not so
flip as it seems, for the poem surely means that God alone
does know when true love underlies and is expressed by
what one might think is only lasciviousness.

His verse of the late forties and early fifties, often occasional and sometimes light, has almost always, subtly or
more obviously, a religious basis: It is recognizable as
Christian poetry. He writes of Eliot, the Christian poet, "on
his sixtieth birthday." And he writes in memory of Charles

Williams, the Christian apologist, in "Memorial for the City," a dense and somewhat difficult poem on the vision of the human city, a place which is the debased version of that City of God cited in his epigraph from the mystic Julian of Norwich. There is a sense of double meaning in these lines about the earthly metropolis, "post-Vergilian," and thus evoking epic meaning but not now heroic, *new* but very old as an idea, *sane* (to medieval theology) and not yet whole or healthy, *sinful* (to the Reformation) and still a shadow of the sacred, *rational* (to the Enlightenment) but lacking perfect reason, *glittering, conscious,* and finally *abolished,* as the barbed wire of the prison or the concentration camp runs through it. Adam's true city home is not yet established. The contrast of the parallel, yet vastly different, cities of God and of man is echoed in the rhyming and contrasting verbal pairs, *Lord* and *sword, hymns* and *limbs, reason* and *treason.* This extraordinary verbal and intellectual performance ends with a cryptic-seeming fourth section written in the first person. The reader may wonder, who are the *I* and *me* in these lines? Possibly the answer is implicit in the fact that this is a memorial not only for the city but for Williams, whose *Descent of the Dove,* a work so important for Auden as a source of his conversation, is about the Paraclete, the Holy Ghost. "I know a ghost" is one phrase casually thrown in as a clue in these last lines. It is the Spirit to whom the "fifth word" on the cross, "I thirst," has been permitted, an expression that serves as a "stumbling block to the stoics" because it admits and indeed insists upon the new Adam's, the incarnate Being's, physical need. (The Paraclete is mediator between divine and temporal, joining spirit and flesh.) This poem about civilization as a radically imperfect trope for the order of a Heavenly City is in the spirit of and, at last, on the Spirit of Charles Williams.

Other poems of the period invoke other names and places: a canon of Christ Church, Oxford, on his eightieth birthday; Mozart, along with a number of Auden's friends and familiar locations; and, in "Precious Five," the person-ified senses. In most one finds a mood of awe and finally the utterance of a blessing.

Like Milton, however (a poet whose influence could not be escaped but one whom, Auden was certain, he would have disliked intensely in person), he frequently reverted from Christian to classical and pagan topics, while treating these myths in an essentially Christian way. The title poem of his volume *The Shield of Achilles* provides a grim and striking modern version of Homer's passage, in Book Eigh-teen of the Iliad, where Hephaestos makes the magnificent shield that pictures life and landscape heroically human and majestically divine. In Homer the shield becomes a visual and real epitome of the whole epic. In Auden it is trans-formed into a sorrier thing. Thetis, the mother of Achilles, looks over the shoulder of the metalworker god and sees, to her dismay, that he can represent now not a "well-governed" city or a fruitful scene but rather wilderness without a neighborhood. Here, in the dull and dismal present day, there is no dance and music, but there is, again, barbed wire, brutality. Here, there is reenactment not of Hellenic but of Christian mythic acts, as "three pale fig-ures" are bound to posts set "upright" on the ground: These are at once concentration camp victims, prisoners, and the three figures on the crosses of Golgotha. A posthe-roic religious sense of a very unheroic fallen world informs, at last, even the reading of Homer. The slayer Achilles is reduced in our eyes. He will "not live long."

A lover of the Greek and Roman classics—he edited and wittily introduced a collection of classical writing—Auden often tries to give the apparently distant and grandiose a common, current meaning. In "Secondary Epic," on the Aeneid, Virgil is told, no, he cannot fairly predict the fu-ture, as that work has predicted the founding of Rome—but not its later Catholic significance. He does not debunk history in "Makers of History," "The History of Science," and "The History of Truth," but he perceives how difficult it is in this age to accept unquestionably the great assured truths of a historic "ago." His "Homage to Clio," the classical Muse of history (it was written in 1955 but was to become the title poem for his 1960 collection), pays its respects to the chronicle, to recollection, and to gossip, and concludes that facts both good and bad are to be kept in memory, although they do not alone make up the epic poetry of Homer and Virgil or his own nonheroic work. Does Clio bless the poets? It seems unlikely that she reads them, and why should she? This is a wry invocation of the Muse, very different from, say, Milton's.

Poetry and plain historical truth are definitely distinguished one from the other in "The Truest Poetry is the Most Feigning."[6] The Christian answer to "How much do you love me?" should be just so much, no more. But poets are not priests, and they must use words playfully, artfully. As the poet said to a class of women students, if a young man writes you a love poem that is a good poem, he is probably more interested in poetry about the beloved than in the beloved, or the real you. The man who would very shortly after this time reject much of his earlier work as dishonest now writes that, far from being sincere, the poet may change his verses to his "dear," if political conditions demand it, into lines praising a "Generalissimo." The message sounds cynical—and some critics found its apparent triviality distasteful—but the true point is that art is artifice while truth or orthodoxy is another matter; yet, unlike Plato, who condemned poets as liars, and like Browning with his lie like truth, Auden concludes by suggesting that behind the false front is the true, veiled, meaning: The last word of the poem is *reticence*.[7]

He was reticent about his private life, his deepest sexual and religious feelings, but he did not disavow them or attempt disguises so much as he gave them imaginative and indirect expression. This feigning could be more true than naked truth. In *Horae Canonicae*, the series on canonical hours observed by monastic orders, Auden objectifies attitudes that are personal, pious, moral, but the result is not straightforward confession any more than it is homily. "Prime," "Terce," "Sext," "Nones," "Vespers," "Compline," and "Lauds" are times of day, times of life, times in history, and they imply times in the personal history of the writer. "Prime" marks the dawn, and the creation or beginning of time, the creation specifically of Adam, the self. Yet, in this time of Eden and awakening there is anticipation, anxious as well as hopeful, of the living and the dying that the day to come requires. This section begins with a reference to Virgil's two gates of sleep, the horn and ivory portals "of the mind," one leading to the underworld, the other giving access to false dreams (and an exit for Aeneas); the simultaneous opening of the two indicates that in the birth of humankind death is implicit. That Christian idea anticipates the hours and eras to come: "Terce," nine in the morning and the early part of an ordinary life; "Sext," noon, when civilization is developing with all its concomitant sophisticated evils; "Nones," three in the afternoon and the time of guilt, remorse; "Vespers," six o'clock, the period of reflection upon a daytime of doubt, betrayal, alienation; "Compline," nine in the evening, when day is passing and men ask if they and their times can be saved; and "Lauds," midnight, final hour of prayer that is both lone and communal.

In the last words of "Terce," the poet extends and specifies the sense of human life's having to be a constant dying. The common person's common day is Friday, and it seems to end well enough because it has been, all in all, a "good Friday." Here the true nature of the work becomes explicit: Its center and subject is the three-hour period—the hours on the cross—of Good Friday, which is the central and most sacred moment in the Christian day and year. The paradox of "good Friday," a time that is altogether good because it is altogether bad, a time of greatest suffering that gives birth to greatest joy, is parallel with the initial idea that new life implies death as death brings life again.

"Sext" or midday is the moment when civilizing rules and rites are developed. In the time of Christ, it was the moment when the temple priests began the sacrificing of the Passover sheep. Without such a vocation as this, without the devotion of maker, healer, priest, there would be no city, no civilization, and there would be "no agents" to accomplish "this death," the noontime crucifixion. The acknowledged need to be civilized, follow a rite, work and worship as a crowd, as a community, implies in "this world" the eruption of a brutality that civilization is precisely designed to control. These lines end on the cross with the last word, *dying*.

"Nones" has been thought by many readers to be the most powerful of the sequence, and there is reason to suppose that Auden thought it the most important. (The parts were written between 1949 and 1954, and "Nones," dated 1950, came chronologically in the middle of the period, as it comes—being part four—in the middle part of the *Horae*.) It begins with a reference to the foretelling, by hermits, the sybil, and by chance—the child's chance rhyme of *will* and *kill*—rather than Isaiah, of today's event. Now it is over; the blood has dried already. Now, alone, we wonder what to do until the night; we are only our lone selves, realizing that there *is* work to do, the work of restoring an order we "try to destroy," and have today tried to destroy. The order we shattered is our own order, and the flesh we pierced is "our own wronged flesh." The use of *we*, identifying all humankind with those who cried out in the past, and, again today, in the voices of the whole congregation during the Anglican Good Friday reenactment, who cry out, "Crucify him," anticipates the penitent communal prayer with which this whole work ends. "Nones" itself ends with the awed creatures, hawk, hen, bug, deer, more innocent than human beings, looking at the spot of the sacrifice. For us, still, the meaning of the "mutilated" body awaits to haunt the idle dreams and nightmares of the day's hours and the night's.

The next part, "Vespers," is in prose and is deliberately prosaic, almost flat, a moment of reflection. It returns to Adam, now with Eve, his sexual complement and opposite, and finds in their uneasy "citizenship"—for the city, the state, have their beginning in the institution of marriage—the beginning of that universal human experience, the discovery of how much others *are* other, standing in contrast and opposition to self. One is type, the other antitype; one is aesthetic, imaginative, bourgeois, the other political, rational, proletarian; one longs for Arcadia or Eden, the other for Utopia or the withering away of the state. So the first one dreams of an impossible past to be reached by means of fantasy, and the second one dreams of an impossible future to be reached by means of revolution. Finally, the two must meet and realize that each is a hidden half of the other. At this point both remember "our victim," Christ in the guise of any "Sin Offering"—the first reminds the second of His innocence, the second reminds the first of His blood—without whose brutal death and innocent suffering no secular civilization, no dream of Arcadia or Utopia, would exist.

At nine o'clock, at "Compline," sleep is already approaching: The body is drowsy and cannot completely remember what happened between twelve and three, the death on the cross; but the heart confesses that reality, and the stars sing of it in unexpected "hilarity," separating themselves from the body's here and now, protecting it from being fully and terribly "shaken awake." The bodily being often forgets the body sacrificed. Yet, at last, it may awaken and "join the dance" of which the constellations sing, a dance around "the abiding tree." Those are the final words of these unrhymed and somehow regularly irregular lines. The tree takes us back to Eden but is as well the rood, the cross, as it is a tree, and the axletree upon which the universe rotates.

"Lauds," coming at midnight, marks the actual beginning of the day, for the moment after twelve is A.M., is ante meridiem. The daily cycle has begun again. The end is the commencement. In the first draft of these lines, the initial and the final tercets conclude with a refrain, "Day breaks for joy and sorrow." The rest of the verse is in couplets. The later and much stronger version changes that refrain, which becomes constant so that all the stanzas are tercets, to *In solitude, for company.*" This, finally, is a prayer as much of blessing as of asking, blessing the temporal world of hours in which one person, guilty, penitent, and incorrigibly natural, is alone and yet part of "the People." For prayer is at last both single and common, an act of the community. The conclusion of a Sequence upon Good Friday as the terrible heart of a mystery now becomes, with the reserved Good Friday sacrament, a prayer at Communion. At the Eucharistic moment, the moment of communion, Eden is recalled and the day once more breaks.

Auden's religious poetry, then, is personal and singular while it appeals to a common experience. His secular and, again, personal verse also refers to people in general, to the whole world of others. When, in 1958, he bid farewell to his summer home on Ischia, he made the "Good-Bye to the Mezzogiorno" a comment on the range of European styles, the difference and the relationship between North and South. The Italian South is the poet's own "otherwhere," the place where he encounters the "anti-self" that proves to be so much a part of himself and yet one that is alien; for this is a place where he cannot continue to live. He has, literally, to return to his "gothic North." He has hoped to learn from what he is not now just what he might become, but what he learns is that northerners in the south are likely to "spoil," and so he must now say good-bye to beautiful Italy, gratefully, blessing it, yet going home.

The poetry that Auden wrote after returning to his northern origins, to Oxford and New York in winter and Austria every summer, has to do with nature and his own nature, places and his own place, love and his own loved ones. These are largely poems of occasion again, and they have a freshness, a variety, and a degree of intellectual seriousness as well that contradict the too-frequent assertion of his diminishing powers.

His "Dame Kind," using for title a phrase, a name that Auden already several times has invoked, is about nature, physical and specifically sexual, and although it celebrates that nature—"She *is* our Mum"—it denies it the primary place of Robert Graves's White Goddess. He was firm in resisting anthropological reductionism which found a single simple principle of Being in all religion. Once, at a lecture given by the popular writer on myth, Joseph Campbell, who argued (for example) blandly that Christ and Buddha were identical because both had spears used against them, although in Buddhism the spears were transformed into flowers, Auden exclaimed quite loudly that on Good Friday the spears were real ones. Dame Kind is mother, Nature, bawd, and inspirer, but not the Almighty, any more than Buddha is Jesus.

Other poems of 1959, "Reflections in a Forest," "Hands," "The Sabbath," and "Walks," are formal, thoughtful, reflective, often light in tone. The most solemn, the most moving, is "Friday's Child," written in memory of Dietrich Bonhoeffer, the German theologian killed by the Nazis in 1945. It is a Kierkegaardian and therefore existential comment on the freedom of the human will, freedom to act in brutality as if a god, and freedom to suffer as God has on the cross at the Friday sacrifice, and as Bonhoeffer has, suffering martyrdom.

The last part of *Homage to Clio,* given as "Addendum" and entitled "Academic Graffiti" ("*In Memoriam Ogden Nash*") is just for fun. It consists of very short rhymes, mostly four-liners in some kind of rough dimeter or trimeter, on eminent writers, musicians, and notables; they are nonsense verses that poke fun at poetry as if to say that one need not be altogether or always solemn.

It appears that by the very late fifties and, especially, the early sixties, the poet was moving indoors. His interest in locations now becomes an interest in places to inhabit, in parts of the house. The sequence finally called *Thanksgiving for a Habitat* makes clear this tending to fall into domesticity. These poems on architecture or the "Geography of the House" (the title of the sixth one, dedicated to Christopher Isherwood) are not among his greatest, but they are among the more charming of his personal verses. The fact that they are inscribed to intimate friends may suggest the intimate and easy nature of the writing. At the end of his fifties he is settling down and settling in.

Most of the verses he composed in his last years can be described as occasional: They concern himself and persons, places, moments, in his own life. One of them, entitled simply, "You," is an address of the self to the self, or of the mind to the body. The poems on places to which he traveled include "Iceland Revisited" and "On the Circuit," a partly complaining, largely grateful, and wholly witty account of his reading tours that ends by blessing the U.S.A., "so rich." He very much appreciated the money he was paid for making appearances and reciting his work. There is indeed a good deal of wit in this poetry—it includes three "Posthumous Poems" written a half-dozen and more years before his death—and there is a paying of tribute to people he loved. The "Eleven Occasional Poems" memorialize and celebrate the lives of John F. Kennedy, Josef Weinheber (who had died in 1945), Elizabeth Mayer (on her eightieth birthday), Nevill Coghill (on his retirement in 1966), Marianne Moore (when she, in turn, reached the age of eighty), as well as several others; they include toasts to Christ Church, Oxford, and to the retiring Oxford professor, William Empson. Never displaying sentimentality, these are all expressions of sentiment.

Some of the work of this period displays anything but sentimentalism, verging indeed on the crotchety. But he will indulge his crotchets only up to a point. "City Without Walls," a poem that would lend its title to the 1969 collection, is about the vulgarity and violence, the danger and decay of contemporary life. There seems to be no bounded, ordered city, or *civitas,* in the world today. The indictment of this world goes on at length, in a series of five-line stanzas. The cadence of these apparently tight or walled-in verses is in fact loose and irregular, for their subject is the sense of a "Nothing" in the existence of "nobodies." Then the form changes to three-line, tighter, and yet rhythmically more free stanzas which reveal that these are night-time thoughts: "I was thinking at three A.M." Another voice interrupts the thought, accusing thinker and speaker of playing at satire and dire prophecy, of enjoying bitter reflections. Finally, a third voice is heard, telling the Jeremiah-Juvenal and his critic to go to sleep: They will both feel better at breakfast. This is the point beyond which aging disillusion does not go; Auden's sense of humor stops him short with the prospect of morning and food. Possibly the second and third voice are to be identified with Orlan Fox and Chester Kallman. The first voice is the poet's own, using his own familiar themes of sad change, the death of civility, his familiar imagery of the human city, and finally responding to his own dear friends.

Life and death, time and change, persons and places, make up until the end the topics of his poetry. One late poem is "Amor Loci," "love of places." Another significant title is "In Due Season." There is throughout this verse, as well, a clear religious feeling that seems now calm and assured. It goes along with the lightheartedness that even his poetry on age, loneliness, and dying can display. A piece written in 1969, "The Ballad of Barnaby," seems to be a version of the *Jongleur de Notre Dame.* Light and charming in its piety, it was published as a sort of broadside on blue paper with fine, droll illustrations by Edward Gorey.

The knowledge of age and death fills a good deal of the later lyric verse, but it is never morbid, never cheerless. In his "Prologue at Sixty," he looks forward with a lively interest to the "eighth day," the timeless time beyond, when he can "accomplish my corpse at last"; in "Epistle to a

Godson" (for Phillip Spender), he is flattered by the boy's having given thanks for a "boozy godfather," one who knows he needs an annual checkup; his tribute to David Protech, "The Art of Healing" (Protech was a Boston medical man as well as a part of the literary life, one who had lived recklessly—he was at Auden's all-night party in Northampton—and died young), ends with "affection" and "praise." Among Auden's latest poems are "Doggerel by a Senior Citizen" and "Old People's Home," in which he wishes for a quick and happy sleep to be given to a friend, a woman now exhausted and decayed. But through all this awareness of aging and mortality there can be heard the note of buoyant thankfulness. "Thank You, Fog" voices his gratitude for what he has been, where he has been, and where he is, again in his own native Britain and at peace. The final poems in Mendelson's definitive edition are "A Thanksgiving"—to Hardy, Thomas, Frost, Yeats, Graves, Brecht, Kierkegaard, Charles Williams, Lewis, Horace, and Goethe—and "A Lullaby," a bright and lively comment on how age reverts to youth, which ends *Sleep, Big Baby, sleep your fill.*"

At his death, Wystan Hugh Auden was remembered as a great lyric poet, although his poetic drama and his criticism are of great, perhaps of equal, importance. When the news of his death was reported by American radio, a listening group in a New England drawing room heard it with shock and sadness; then three of them, the poet Richard Wilbur, the critic Alfred Kazin, and his wife, the novelist Ann Birstein, said in one voice, "Earth, receive an honoured guest."[8] That immediate response, quoting one of Auden's finest lines in the elegy for Yeats, summed up the memory of the poet and his lyric vocation.

3

Plays

Auden's dramatic work is largely but not entirely collaborative, largely but not entirely poetic. Most of it includes playfulness of both plot and language. The great appeal of the theatre for him seems to be that it allows for "playing," that is, for acting roles and at the same time taking part in a dialogue or charadelike game. There is always something deeply serious about the game, but the serious themes are often dealt with wryly, sometimes in a flippant or a joking tone, just as the dramatic plots display surprises, tricks, deliberate and dreamlike distortions. Whether producing allegories, film scripts, plays for the church and theatre, or libretti, the author refuses to be either dully literal or pompous.

His first important dramatic attempt, the one-act *Paid on Both Sides,* comes from the period 1928–1929, and it clearly displays the influence of John Layard's ideas about physical, mental, and moral health, the first two being determined by the last. It concerns a feud between two families, the Nowers and the Shaws. The play begins with the birth of John Nower just after his father has been killed by the enemy Shaws; we then move quickly to a period some years later when, a young man, John is firmly intent upon revenge. He traps and kills one of the Shaw agents. Immediately afterward he falls into troubled sleep, and the action now is that of a dream-play. In the young Nower's dream, he is at once two persons, his conscious self and his enemy, the Spy, whom he accuses. This dream, then, dramatizes La-

yard's and Auden's belief that each person is his own enemy
and that suppression of the anti-self is a source of neurotic
illness. In the dreaming state, John again murders the Spy,
who is brought back to life by a comic "Doctor." This
whole sequence is a kind of trial. Identified as Father
Christmas, the judge of the trial reveals the truth, that John
is a divided personality who denies himself the possibility of
loving by denying the other part of himself. The vindictive
mother, the enemy Shaws, John's long-suffering fiancée
Anne, and John himself are all caught in a destructive cycle, one that at last is starkly tragic. The work concludes
with the words of a chorus, echoing the chorus of Greek
tragedy as it comments on the loss of lands, loved ones, and
life, all the result of inner discord, of a self-betrayal.

Brilliant as many passages are in this kaleidoscopic
drama, with its odd and dazzling imagery, the result is often obscure. Auden himself recognized and regretted the
fact, writing in a journal that he had been too lazy to clar-
ify his ideas so as to avoid that obscurity. Already, in 1929,
he felt the obligation to make sense to a general audience.
That was the purpose of the theatre; but he was not yet
able, for all his skill at words, to achieve a complete and
producible play.

Dramatic form continued to fascinate him, and he returned to it repeatedly throughout his career, with increas-
ing success. Yet he had to work for directness and clarity.
His next, half-serious, half-joking dramatic effort, called
"The Reformatory" in its first form, and then revised and
entitled *The Enemies of a Bishop, or Die When I Say
When,* was in that revision a collaborative effort with Isherwood. They called it, ambitiously, "A Morality in Four
Acts," but it was as much as anything else a working-out of
their schoolboylike fantasies and private jokes. In it, verse
and straight dialogue alternate as part of the wordplay and
horseplay. The main character is a young man named Bicknell (Auden's mother's family name) whose brother is the
governor of a reform school for boys, and the cast includes

as well a Bishop Law—the voice of law—two boys who escape from the reformatory, and, among other figures, one called the Spectre, who is Robert Bicknell's anti-self, whom Robert murders at the end as Nower killed the spy in Auden's earlier play. The setting is a gothic area called Mortmere, suggesting something like dead waters; this is an imaginary spot that Isherwood and Auden invented in their boyish fantasies, a spot both fascinating and fearsome, where very odd people behave very oddly, in fact, perversely. The perversities are specifically sexual. The work was never produced and probably was not written to be staged.

Slightly later and certainly more serious pieces, *The Dance of Death* (1933) and *The Dog Beneath the Skin* (1935), the latter another work of collaboration with Isherwood, were, however, written for the theatre, and they were in fact produced. Both were published as well, and the dates cited here are those of publication.

The theatrical producer Rupert Doone first suggested to Auden his writing a play based on the medieval *danse macabre* (five years later he would write a poem with just that title); the result was *The Dance of Death*, which was published in 1933 and presented by the Group Theatre in 1934. The play was intended to demand a great deal of audience participation. That and the fact that it is flatly political in argument make it less impressive on the page than it may have been, with singing, dancing, and the parodying of musical comedy routine, upon the stage. Its stated subject is the death wish and the dying of the middle class, and its line is clearly Marxist. At the end, Karl Marx appears to speak this message. The medieval motif is used, then, for parody, communal theatre, and propaganda, all set to jazz rhythms. The work seems alternately grim and comic, preachy and wisecracking. As a theatrical event it appears to have been at least engaging. As poetry it seemed flat to most critics, who tended to regard it as Auden's poorest published work.

This verse play's relative weakness suggests a reality that
the writer would later acknowledge, that he was not essentially a political creature, and that he was surest when he
took not a single, simple position, but when he observed
the always complex and often inscrutable questions of individual and social life. The death wish of a whole class is too
pat and general as an idea for him to deal with it persuasively.

Even though *The Dog Beneath the Skin* is again a political and even a polemical play, it has more range, more sub-
tlety and wit. Both Isherwood and Auden were interested in
questions of health and neurosis, of love as a possibility distinct from negative self-love, and as public morality. Their
method in this play, a fanciful realizing of metaphor—for
"dog" means underdog, determined and faithful creature,
and finally the unreflective animal nature beneath each human appearance—allows for that combination of high seriousness and fun and games that is the mark of Auden's best
writing.[1]

The narrative is that of a quest. A young man, Alan Norman, is chosen by chance to seek out the missing son of a
local landowner; the chance, however, is propitious because
Alan will prove to be the one person, ultimately set apart
from other villagers, to undertake that search. He seeks
through a maze of places, from a park to a hospital to a
lunatic asylum to a luxury hotel. The various settings allow
for parodic treatment of egoism, self-induced illness, the
pride of the surgeon (whose patient dies), and the smugness
of the heartless capitalist. On this quest, Alan is accompanied by a dog. This is the title's "dog beneath the skin,"
and the denouement, which reveals his human as well as
doggy nature, is the answer to the subtitle's question,
"Where is Francis?"

The son and heir being sought is Sir Francis Crewe: The
name might finally be taken to suggest Saint Francis with
his love for simple animal life as well as the common condition of the honest man, like that of a crew member on the

ship of state. For near the end of the play it is revealed that
the dog is Sir Francis in disguise. But before that revelation
there must be a story unfolded. The chorus and semichorus
sing, ominously, of this time and place, and they continue
to be heard in commentary on the action throughout the
play. In contrast to their choral prescience, the confusion of
ordinary people produces a babble; for these are the trivial,
gossiping, and backbiting common folk who are not in fact
honest men and women, but whose diurnal existence is disordered, hardly shipshape. Their vicar and the gentry, General Hotham, his wife, and Iris Crewe, appear as merely
pompous, certainly unable to guide wisely. Pressan Ambo is
a village that represents the purposeless vanity of a world.
When the vicar chooses one to undertake a quest, he does
so by picking, blindfolded, a piece of paper from a hat. And
when Alan is about to set off, the one impassioned message
given him by the crazed Mildred Luce, whose son was
killed by Germans in the First World War, is to annihilate
those Germans and their land. In Yeats's words, only the
worst-intentioned are "full of passionate intensity."

The mysterious dog goes with Alan, to follow him
throughout his quest—for what the quester seeks abroad is
what he has that is unrecognized. Other characters who enter in scene after scene serve as types; the two journalists
first met on a Channel steamer, who are the "inside" people; the King of Ostnia who personally, politely, and with
religious ritual shoots and kills the predictable rebels
against his law and order; the bawds and pimps who sell
gratification—sex of all sorts, and drugs; the Westland lu-
natics in Act Two who are madly enthusiastic followers of
a dictatorial leader, and the financier met on a train—he is
always on the move—who, with a pitiless greed that makes
him both lonely and pitiable, tries to buy loyalty, offering
poor Alan vast sums of money to work for him; the young
and old egoists in Paradise Park; and the callous medical
staff of the hospital.

Act Two ends with a dialogue between Alan's right foot, speaking in cultivated tones, and his left foot, whose language is Cockney. (A note suggests that this dialogue should be omitted in performance, and it might prove somewhat difficult to stage.) Act Three begins in a luxury hotel, the Nineveh, and now the persons are not only human types of madness, selfishness, and foolishness, but yet more frightening figures, nightmare figures at last. For the Nineveh Hotel comes to seem like hell on earth, a hell of unreality, illusion, nightmare. Here people chatter mindlessly, "chorus girls" sing and dance grimly, and there is nothing but facade. The women, young and old, who provide entertainment are deliberately and ironically called "girls," and one might say that Auden and Isherwood are making a feminist attack on sexual exploitation—rather, dehumanization—when one of them is sold to a diner who plans to have her stewed for his meal, her fingernails to be served separately. He carries her off, and she makes no complaint. After the chorus line, another perversion of entertainment is introduced with "Destructive Desmond," who burns the manuscript pages of Shakespeare and slashes a Rembrandt to bits, to the audience's delight. But in a third scene we encounter the most grotesque persons and situations. Alan himself is transformed into a fool, and worse, totally self-deceived and perhaps temporarily mad, when he has a glimpse of the beautiful star Lou Vipond. She is described as irresistible and heartless, but it soon appears that "she" has no human existence at all; rather, she is a shopwindow dummy. Alan makes love to this form and, to gain some response, dashes behind it and speaks in a falsetto voice the words of love he wants to hear. This is the projection of the self into an object, the fantasy that is falsely called love: Such mad "love" is no longer even lust. Then, when humiliation and ruin threaten Alan, the dog throws off his skin, reveals himself as Sir Francis, and devises the hero's escape.

Yet all the self-deluding and insane qualities that have
been seen upon the quest have at last to come home when
Alan himself comes home, only to discover that the general
and the vicar are militarizing a docile village population,
that Iris Crewe has eagerly engaged herself to a munitions
maker, and that simple life in quiet England is susceptible
to every moral and psychological infection that we have
seen abroad. The vicar speaks eloquently, even persuasively—Auden reissued the passage as "Depravity: A Sermon" in his *Collected Poetry*, adding a note on how it
demonstrates the replacement of Conscience by a smug "my
conscience"—until one realizes that in fact he is urging village boys to form a Fascist amateur army.[2] Sir Francis, who
will be joined by Alan and some other villagers in leaving
the village, now reveals his disguise, a disguise that itself
reveals. It has revealed to him what it is like to be "underneath," an inferior; and it reveals as well his own basic nature. The conclusion of quest and masquerade is a moral,
public, and at last a political statement. Francis declares
that he will join the "other side," opposing the villagers
who now appear as Fascists—and who themselves wear
masks of beasts much less attractive than a dog's skin.

The play was published in 1935 and performed in 1936,
when Mussolini was in power and Hitler was seizing
power, and when Fascism was a virulent force in Britain
itself. Its sense of urgency is not at all a matter of some chic
quasi-Communist pose.

Yet this was and is a clever and a funny play. It can be
called musical comedy with a message, or, rather, with several messages, for it is concerned with the relationships that
link illness, extreme neurosis, economic injustice, political
repression. Auden included verses from it in his later collections of poetry, suggesting that he himself saw the work as
a successful combination of poetry and drama.

The lightness and liveliness of *The Dog Beneath the Skin*
(the lightness, that is, of touch but not of topic or at least of
tone) is reflected in one critic's comment that it begins in

the vein of Gilbert and Sullivan. Even the pro-Fascist vicar's sermon has some element of the comic clergyman in earlier spoofs—in, especially, Wilde. Auden's and Isherwood's next play, *The Ascent of F6*, has almost none of that quality. Its subtitle is "A Tragedy in Two Acts." It is as Freudian as it is Marxist, with an Oedipal central character, and certainly more tragic than parodically comic.

The Ascent itself is a darkly ironic title. A compulsive desire to ascend, to rise above the mundane, leads here only to a fall. The pride engendered by a sense of limitation and self-doubt, the overweening because unself-certain pride of Lucifer, Adam, and Oedipus is the pride of Ransom in this play, and it causes his climbing, then his fall.

Yet Ransom is another figure who must undertake a quest, and the quest continues to attract Auden as a theme—the quest that may be necessary, inescapable, in some sense admirable, while it is the result of a neurotic and finally a self-immolating drive. The authors' and the audience's response to Ransom must be ambivalent, for he is both strong in resolve and weak in personality, both a courageous seeker and an escapist, overcompensating for the Oedipal guilt that he cannot really escape. If this is a problem in the play, it is less serious than the lack of total coherence; for here again there are versions of the confused common people in the audience, and they do not seem to be linked very effectively with the main action.

The play begins with Michael Ransom reading Dante and questioning the great poet's knowledge and virtue—his ideas, that is, of virtue and knowledge. It is immediately clear that Ransom feels some sense of inadequacy, as he declares that the unborn are happy who cannot cry "Mama"; and his very phrasing implies the psychosexual block he suffers. When the voices of his friends Shawcross and Gunn call to him, he goes to start on a climbing tour of the Lake District, a first and minor self-justifying journey. His need to be the extraordinary man is at once contrasted, in the next section, with the ordinariness of Mrs. and Mr. A., whose dull dialogue ends the first scene.

In a number of ways *The Ascent of F6* does resemble the earlier Auden-Isherwood play, even if it lacks the darkly comic quality of *The Dog* (one character in it, Gunn, begins to recite a bawdy limerick but is cut off); here, the quest again involves the fictional land of Ostnia, and the play includes odd and disembodied stage voices as well as a chorus. The political comment is more specific, perhaps, in its Marxist message—although the last line in *The Dog Beneath the Skin* is in fact a paraphrase of Marx, "To each his need: from each his power"—but both are political as well as moral and psychological in message. Michael Ransom's twin brother, in this play's second scene, along with the newspaper magnate, a crusty general, and Lady Isabel, all staunch Tories, can be taken to represent the greedy colonialism and arrogance of an established order. Their motive for wanting the Sudoland mountain F6 to be scaled is a desire to overawe and keep in subjection the native workers on British coffee plantations.

When James proposes the climb to his brother, Michael Ransom refuses. He changes his decision only after their mother enters scene and speaks to him persuasively. She confides how she has always known, while she seemed to favor James, that quiet Michael was the strong son, James the shallow one who needed to be flattered. In effect, she is appealing to his strength now, and at the same time to his weakness, his deep need to be reassured of her love in order to believe in himself as a man. It is weakness because this dominating form of maternal love can cripple but not nourish. Yet the appeal is irresistible.

Michael at last agrees to undertake the quest, to make the ascent. The second act takes us to the haunted mountain itself. Here the special themes and interests of Auden become clear: his fascination with the moral implications of a rugged topography, his idea of the demon that is an unrecognized and self-destroying self, and his profound religious

feeling, already displayed in the person of an abbot. If
Marx, Freud, and Layard are forces in the play, the whole
work is not only a didactic presentation but a probing of
the human spirit, of the spiritual. When all the mountaineers look into a mirrorlike crystal belonging to the native
monks, each sees something—some thing—unsettling, of
his inner self. For Michael Ransom this is the temptation to
save humankind, to be a Messiah and thus, in the Christian
framework, God Himself. The abbot tells Ransom that his
vision represents the presence of this haunted mountain's
demon. But it is too late for Michael to resist and renounce
his terrible quest.

Michael Ransom dies on the summit of F6, as have all
the other mountaineers. When his spectre returns to haunt
his brother James there is the first in a series of reversals.
James is defeated, as in a chess game where the other characters are pawns. But then Michael is again confronted by
the abbot in a dreamlike scene, is tried by the living and the
dead, and fully recognizes his own pride and moral failure.
Ironically, the work ends with voices praising the dead hero
for his courage, sensitiveness, selfless patriotism. All these
qualities, valued by the others as they serve the cause of
Empire, of colonial exploitation and greed, have been recognized by Ransom as signs of his possession by his own
demon.

The last of the plays at which Auden worked in the forties is the weakest and the least remembered. *On the Frontier: A Melodrama in Three Acts* might well have been
impressive, for as its title indicates it has again to do with
location, and specifically a location that often appears in
the poetry—the frontier, borderline, or crucial place and
time. But this anti-Fascist drama is so flatly political and
polemical that it achieves little vitality even as melodrama.
Once again it evokes the imaginary countries Ostnia and
Westland, and it has a chorus of prisoners, soldiers, working people, who speak the basic message. It was produced

by the Group Theatre in 1938. The poet-dramatist himself did not regard it highly and did not keep any part of it in his later published volumes.

From now on, his theatrical work would be written not for the conventional stage but for other media or other kinds of presentation. In 1940 his radio play *The Dark Valley* was broadcast, with Dame May Whitty performing the monologue as an old and lonely woman who is about to kill her goose ("that Laid the Golden Egg") while she comments on the world's landscape and what Gerard Manley Hopkins called its inscape. This fantasy script is not in print except for two lyrics that were included in it, "Eyes Look into the Well" and "Lady, Weeping at the Crossroads."

In 1941 and 1942 Auden was at work on a Nativity play dedicated to his mother, who had just died. This is *For the Time Being* ("A Christmas Oratorio"); it is one of his great works. It combines history, the biblical past, with the idiom of the present in a way that seems surprising, even startling, but does so with great effect. In the letter to his father explaining this mode of telling the story the author observed that it was the practice of medieval play- and picture-makers to show the people in that Christmas story as contemporaries in speech and dress, as the people of "now." (Often the result is anachronism, as when a shepherd, before the birth of Christ, can casually swear "by Our Lady.") Auden's very title implies a double sense of time, identifying the birth that was, almost two thousand years ago, with the Christmas that is, today. He does not use the curious rhetoric of Milton in the Nativity Ode, or of Hopkins at the end of the "Heraclitean Fire" by juxtaposing tenses past and present, but he makes his Joseph a distinctly modern figure sitting in a bar, his shepherds simple rural proletarians, his Herod a civil servant, and his soldiers wisecracking army buddies.

The work begins with the words of Chorus and Semi-Chorus and in the season of Advent. The allusions are, ap-

propriately for a classical chorus, to Caesar and the
Empire. Yet the choruses, the Narrator, and the rest remain
part of a present-day world, as we realize when that Narrator speaks with foreboding of "the political situation."
This is, after all, an anticipation of Christmas in wartime.
It is also the anticipation of a distressing event, for the Nativity must be just that, and even an "Abomination"[3] to
those who live in an old order. At Advent one is made again
to realize that divine Incarnation is madness to Greek and
Roman as it is blasphemy to the people of the place where
it occurs. "The Real," according to a recitative, "is what
will strike you as really absurd."

In "The Annunciation," four faculties speak: Intuition (a
dwarf), Feeling (a nymph), Sensation (a giant), and
Thought (a fairy). Their speech echoes and adds to the
words of the chorus and the recitative preceding them: People are "alone" in a "dreadful wood," but "the garden"
into which women and men cannot enter "is the only place
there is." The faculties describe the various arid landscapes
of this world, alien to the Garden with its "everlasting
fountain"—plain, meadow, river, valley, and, worst vision
of all, the emptiness, the "wide omission" that is "no
ground" as envisioned by Thought. Originally, in the Garden and before the Fall, the faculties were one, but now
they are divided, as the human being in exile is divided. If
the "Garden of Being" is lost, however, it can be re-found.
That, in effect, is the message of Gabriel to the Virgin when
he suggests the parallel between and the radical contrast of
Mary and Eve. Eve, following Adam when he imagined
that he was free and so lost his freedom, chose to deny "the
will of Love." Mary can choose to conceive "the Child who
chooses you." That choice is made, and Solo and Chorus
rejoice along with "number and weight," great and small,
young and old, all "singing and dancing."

If Mary's choice promises redemption from the result of
Eve's choice, Joseph's obedience in "The Temptation of
Saint Joseph" atones for Adam's fall and for his blaming

his disobedience on Eve. Joseph's hard lot is to accept, to trust Mary, lacking any "important and elegant proof." He must "be silent and sit still." The Narrator makes it clear that his atonement is one for masculine pride as well as rebellious will, for objectifying and exploiting women as nurses, servants, "chorus girls" (that phrase glances back to "The Dog Beneath the Skin"), and, perhaps worst of all, inhumanly pure beings: He must learn from Mary's virgin conception that for nature the male is "a non-essential luxury."[4] Joseph is of "the weaker sex." Yet Joseph's position as the patient one is not at all minor. The choruses at the end of this part address Mary and Joseph both, asking their prayers for forgiveness of the intrinsic sinfulness that pious people, married couples, lovers, children, even embryos in the womb, all display.

"The Summons" begins with the Wise Men following the star. This is one of the fairly few passages in Auden that can be taken to show the poetic influence of Eliot, for here as in "The Journey of the Magi" the summons to the Nativity is in large part disquieting: Those summoned have to leave their comfortable lives behind. Each of the Magi here gives a reason for following the star: to discover how to be truthful, how to live, how to love. Together they add these reasons up, and the sum is one reason. They must discover "how to be human." The eastern Wise Men stand in contrast to the mighty western Caesar, who here represents modern authority, technology, and rational order. In a chilling chorus we hear how Caesar, or what earthly power that calls the people together to be registered, has "conquered Seven Kingdoms": the kingdoms of Abstract Idea (under Caesar, language is ruled by grammar and myth is dead), of Natural Cause (now science and technology replace worship and wonder), of Infinite Number (uncertain things are now precisely calculated), of Credit Exchange (we now have credit cards and world trade), of Inorganic Giants (the consumer is served), of Organic Dwarfs (we have medicines and drugs), and of Popular Soul (our opinions are formed and we are entertained). Caesar's manipulative mass media do all of this; "God must be with Him." No, the tone tells us, not God the Father. The section ends with a beautiful chorale, a kind of Paternoster and one of the finest parts of the work, beginning, "Our Father, Whose creative Will/ Asked Being for us all." The verse is formal, sparse, and starkly graceful.

"The Vision of the Shepherds" concerns very common folk who wear "ready-made clothes" and are "ordered about." One might be reminded of the comment by Empson (whom Auden very much admired) in *Some Versions of Pastoral* that the shepherd is the lowest person in human society and, at the same time, the highest figure in the whole scale of things, for the psalmist's Lord is "my Shepherd" and Christ himself is pictured as the "Good Shepherd." The spiritual value of these simple speakers who watch over sheep and are themselves God's sheep amounts to their being able to bear their condition because they know that they are waiting: "something/will happen," although they do not know what, and "we shall hear the Good News." Now a chorus of angels brings that news, and urges them, "Run to Bethlehem." And so they "run to Love." That is, they run to the very source of love, and run to love that source.

"At the Manger," Mary, the Wise Men, and these shepherds join together. The word *love* recurs throughout this part, insistently. Here, too, at the manger, coming to love means coming home. It is no easy return. It has taken time. But "Time is our choice" of a way to love and the reason for love. They are still *in* time, and therefore limited—as those people were in history and these modern versions are in the present. They are not in the timeless Garden. Yet they live and choose to love here, in and for "the time being."

"The Meditation of Simeon" presents that pious old man (who blessed the Christ child in the Temple) as a visionary and, in effect, a theologian, meditating upon the Fall, on necessity and freedom—necessity is freedom to be tempted, freedom is the necessity to have faith—on Christian comedy, and finally, anticipating the development of doctrine, on the Trinity. The latter parts of this prose "meditation" can be read as a critical commentary upon Auden's religious poetry. The ridiculous is no longer ugly as in pagan and heroic life, Simeon realizes, because every person in the new dispensation must be at once heroic and simpleminded, clumsy, foolish: Everyone is infinitely important and yet limited and made buffoonlike by finite and fallen nature. This belief, which is manifested in Christian literature going back at least to Dante, explains Auden's combining of the highest seriousness with wisecracking, his sense of humor that allows him to regard himself as a prophetic voice and at the same time a performing clown. Simeon's insistence, too, upon God's "need of friends," that is, the necessity for a dynamic of love within the divine unity, as well as his awareness of God's catholicity—He is Lord of the Gentiles as well as of Jesus's people—reflects the poet's sense that one must respect and love otherness because it is other.

"The Massacre of the Innocents" begins with a prose soliloquy of troubled Herod, who speaks as a present-day civil servant. A man of great intelligence, he is politically trapped, wanting to make the best of things, reform the state—even while he has to be skeptical about the possibilities—and administer justice. Having done all that he can do, he finds himself in an intolerable position. "I object," he concludes. "I'm a liberal. I want everyone to be happy. I wish I had never been born." In striking contrast to this discourse, the rowdy song of those soldiers who kill the newborn babes is as hearty as it is heartless, mindless as it is gay. George, the "old numero," the "flybynight," who has lived an offhand life of sexal and sordid adventure, is welcomed back to the army just in time "to massacre the Innocents," and it is all quite jolly. Finally, in a poignant and very brief passage of verse, we hear the voice of Rachel, a mother mourning the slain, whose grief is hardly utterable in the silence and the cold.

The last section of the oratorio is "The Flight into Egypt." Entering the alien land, Mary and Joseph hear the "Voices of the Desert" welcoming them to the place of cablegrams, deadly diseases, and casual whoring. When, after this, the Narrator speaks, we realize that the Holy Family has in fact entered the world of today. Christmas is over; "that is that." We put the tree decorations back into boxes, recover from holiday feasting, and go on with our daily work for the time being, "the most trying time of all." The Nativity has been celebrated, Lent is to come, "The Night of Agony," "Good Friday," and finally Easter. In this Egyptian desert of our lives the memory dimly remains, the Virgin and Child and Joseph are dimly present, and we try fitfully and faintly to redeem the desert days from insignificance. The simple concluding chorus, in three tercets, declares that "He is the Way," "the Truth," "the Life" to be "loved in the World of the Flesh"—so that everything "at your marriage" can dance in joy. The Virgin Birth, then, is at last the source for blessing of marriage and fruitfulness.

The Sea and the Mirror might be considered essentially a work of poetry, for it includes a series of splendid lyrics, even though the penultimate part, "Caliban to the Audience," is in prose, and that is the part Auden regarded as by far the most important. The whole work might also be included in Auden's literary criticism: Its subtitle is "A Commentary on Shakespeare's *The Tempest*," it includes references to other Shakespearean plays—the Preface quotes from *Hamlet* and *Lear*—and it is finally concerned with the nature of literary art, of art in general. But its form is dramatic, and it can be described again as an oratorio without music. Written by Auden while he was teaching at Swarthmore, from 1942 to 1944, it was, he thought, his best work to date.

The stage manager's preface ("to the critics") introduces a contrast between art, which exerts the magic power of a circus performance, and the world of fact that Shakespeare in the voice of Prospero has transformed and diminished to "insubstantial stuff" (in the speech that concludes "We are such stuff/As dreams are made on, and our little life/Is rounded with a sleep."). Yet we live in that world of fact, and art cannot satisfactorily resolve the question of how to live in it, cannot alter human circumstance. As Auden writes elsewhere, poetry makes nothing happen.

The first part of the play proper, "Prospero to Ariel," virtually reverses the relationship between those two in Shakespeare's own play. It is Ariel, with his echoing voice and his mirror held up to reveal people to themselves, who influences the master magician—and, oddly, corrupts him with his "charm." For Prospero realizes now that he has not only wrecked his slave Caliban but also "tempted Antonio into treason" by using Ariel's gifts to enchant the other characters so that Antonio and Sebastian remain the sole persons awake in the scene where they plot the death of Alonso. (In this view, then, the magician has tempted his brother to tempt Alonso's brother.) Yet Prospero is glad that he has freed Ariel, as he is glad that his daughter Miranda, in love, no longer pays any attention to him; he suggests that the corrupting power of Ariel's art is also revealing and even perhaps necessary. As a lyric in the midst of this address wittily asserts, the dangerous illusions of magic, song, and poetry both flatter persons and show up their illusions. Still, the finest poetry in this world has to be distorted, untrue; "the way of truth" is "a way of silence."

The second section begins with Antonio's speech, and Antonio provides a series of refrains, in italics, that punctuate the rest. Auden here expresses his belief that the final scenes of *The Tempest,* especially Gonzalo's speech declaring joyously that all of us in the play "have found ourselves" and announcing a happy ending, are false to the whole work and to the real possibility of what poetic magic can achieve. Antonio remains, in this latter-day version, usurper and absolute egoist. If Antonio is still essentially what he was, so, apparently, is Gonzalo. Yes, he recognizes some of his failures, his false eloquence and ineffectiveness, but he continues to declare that all the cast "have been restored to health." The cynical but more terribly deluded Antonio, proud in being alone, laughs at Gonzalo as he mocks the others. Auden is dramatizing his belief in the imperative to know and accept otherness, the moral and mortal danger of asserting oneself as the self-sufficient, the only real person.

In two lines, the minor figures Adrian and Francisco state the simple common-sense attitude of the ordinary creature: Sunbeams are bright, but when pet fish die, "it's madly ungay." This amounts to a "camp" way of saying that life has its picnics and its sadnesses. Antonio scoffs at them, too, and their jingle or playlet; speaking always of himself by his name, as a self-observer, he exults in his own "drama," the play "in his head alone." *Own* and *alone* are, we now realize, the key words he utters, ending each second and fifth line in each quintain of his thought.

Next comes Alonso's section, which is not thought or speech but a letter to his son Ferdinand, to be read after the old king's death. This letter invokes both the sea and the mirror, and provides the first tentative gloss on those images in Auden's title. The sea is a cold nature that is indifferent to kings, a nature which can be beautiful, blank, deadly; and the mirror ("a prince's ornate mirror") briefly suggests the ancient idea—which Shakespeare echoes—of art as the mirror of all life. That mirror "dare not" tell what darkness, the darkness of ocean and desert, can. (The yoking of such different scapes may predict Auden's passage in *The Enchafèd Flood* on both as settings for the lost wanderer or literary nomad.) Kings and princes must beware of pride in their cities, for there is only a small space for "civil pattern" between vague waters and empty stretches of sand. As in *The Tempest*, Alonso is the wise and loving father without many illusions. It may be that he has not even needed to find himself. The unchanged Antonio, who has conspired against this dying monarch, now declares his own "empire," his "diadem." Antonio's pride begins to reveal itself as madness, as megalomania (and the reader may be sent back to Shakespeare to find evidence that this reading of the treacherous usurper can be sustained.)

In a light interlude, the boisterous Master and Boatswain sing of low dives and the whores who solicit there. But they know the facts of life, including the fact of venereal disease—and the fact that "the sea is deep" into which dead bodies are dropped. They seem to yawn and go to sleep: No profound grief or tragedy is for them. Wry Antonio, dismissing them as "nostalgic sailors," sails that deep sea alone, his compass himself.

Sebastian, who appears now, is especially interesting as embodying the author's most personal feelings—and some of this work is as much about Auden's experience of the rift with young Chester Kallman as it is about Shakespeare's people. Sebastian, trembling, is glad that he was not allowed to succumb to temptation and become a murderer, just as Auden told friends later that he was grateful that he could resist the serious temptation to kill Kallman's new lover. It may seem melodramatic, but apparently he contemplated doing just that. Now Antonio the tempter, without regret or gratitude to any other force, gloats that _his_ conscience is his own.

We might expect Trinculo to provide another light interlude. He does not. His jokes that are greeted by laughter, he knows, are the products of sorrow, suffering, terror, and his audience laughs so as not to weep. To this, Antonio responds that he, still all alone, laughs only at a paradox, the paradox that, having spoken to and now speaking of other persons, he is for himself the one and only Person.

The reader may sympathize with that radio producer who wanted to omit Caliban's lengthy prose discourse from a broadcast, and still understand why Auden could react by saying that everything else might be left out but that this is

the crucial section. It is dense and difficult, written in the
style of the later Henry James—the James who dictated
rather than wrote his fiction, just as this is meant to be spoken—and so apparently as inappropriate as possible for the
voice of the grunting animallike Caliban. Certainly this
passage presents an extraordinary contrast to another poet's version, "Caliban Upon Setebos," in which Robert
Browning has the creature speak elliptically, for the most
part omitting the first person pronoun. Like Faulkner's
child Vardaman in the novel *As I Lay Dying*, Auden's Caliban is given language that he could not say—could not,
that is, as Shakespeare's imagined being—but might inco-
herently feel.

He addresses the audience in the theatre; and his discourse is, first, upon the Muse of dramatic poetry. This
Muse can present history and geography as she will, for
hers are not real times and places. She can discipline and
give both order and orders to her Caliban because he is not
Montaigne's real and interesting cannibal. Yet his being
there suggests the gross reality that art must organize and
the danger that such a witch's son may make "a pass at her
virgin self"—that such rough reality in truth may throw
the artist's organization into disarray. The order of the
Muse's art, of the poetic drama, is one to which actual human disorder and distinctions are alien. (There may be a
memory here of what Keats has said about Shakespeare's
"negative capability," entering into the character of Iago as
into that of Imogen, with equal delight and without distinction—for playwright and actor may find Iago at least as
fine a part as Cassio.) And in art—but not in fact—disorder is "tidiable."

Caliban is the savage, and that means that he is the human. Like a small child, he is savage enough to speak directly even when, as now, he mimics the most artful voice;
and Shakespeare himself, a genius by some accident of history, must by his calling speak indirectly, even falsely; when

his Hamlet tells his players that dramatic art holds a mirror up to nature, he misrepresents, for the magic mirror—here, Ariel's mirror—is a way to compose, control, and necessarily distort.

Throughout this address, then, runs the poetic dramatist's sense of his own distorting vocation, his own self-imposed limitations. In a way, this warning to the poet against the poet's pride is Auden's cautionary message to himself. When Caliban speaks to the young men in the audience who have come here to learn the dramatist's, the magician's, craft, the writer behind this speaker may be warning himself of the dangers in that craft; and of course Auden later will renounce a sleight-of-hand brilliance in favor of being simply honest. Yet, all this is said in the most brilliantly elaborate way.

The danger of art as conceived of by the Romantics, finally, seems to be that it will be too certain of itself, too unaware of perplexing common doubts and discords. In his introduction to the Romantic volume in the series of English poets published by Viking, Auden writes that it is all very well for the writer of genius to expound upon mankind's almost divine creativity, but the man in the street cannot live up to that rhetoric. For Caliban, life is a journey like a train ride, and one that can too easily take us away from ourselves and our confusions into a land where we find the Answer—until we are disillusioned and long for a home and childhood that we sentimentalize so that it, too, is unreal. Being certain of a system or a transcendent order means being alienated from unsatisfactory but actual existence—whether the certainty is poetic, like the visionary one of Milton or of Blake or of Yeats, scientific, like the psychoanalytic ones of Freud or of Lane and Layard, political, like the utopian one of Marx, or religious, like the dogmatic schema of even the greatest theologians. Auden's Caliban values existential anxiety, even existential despair more than perfect assurance. Shakespeare's and Ariel's mirror, like those other mirrors, psychic, social, and ecclesiastical, simplifies and distorts just as the playwright's and the poet's drama misrepresents the original drama, pretending to have found Eden and the Answer.

Auden admired *The Tempest* as a great work, and his criticism here is at least partly turned against those earlier critics who see Prospero as either Shakespeare himself making his farewell bow to the theatre he has magically perfected or as the Almighty in disguise restoring this world to harmony. Even so, he finds the happy ending to this tragicomedy too simply comic (in the large and older sense of that word), too poetically good to be true.

Neither Caliban's address nor Ariel's Postscript, to Caliban, is at all easy to fathom and paraphrase. If, in these voices, Auden is breaking with his own earlier poses of moral and political certainty, he is also puzzling through his own sense of the poet's power and false pride. He said that he meant in *The Sea and the Mirror,* by opposing art and reality, to present the Christian as distinct from the Romantic view of drama, poetry, and all the arts. Because the comedy is not achieved here, and although it warns against Romantic pride in human possibilities, the Christian sense of inadequacy, of being comic, ludicrous, now, does not at last deny that mirror and sea, or Ariel and the fish creature, are related. Ariel's words to Caliban are those of a "sworn comrade," and they are words of fraternal love. Art is fascinated, after all, by "drab mortality," is actually in love with it. The faint and sighing echo at the end of each stanza, simply "I," whispers the fragile identity of magical artifact. The oratorio that begins with a magical circus ends with a love song and a sigh.

There are echoes of *For the Time Being* in *The Sea and the Mirror;* the successful ones in Caliban's audience, for example, assert their accomplishments in almost the very words of the earlier chorus, beginning "Great is Caesar." The essential quality that these two oratorios have in common is an insistence upon time as real, place as definite, in a disorderly order still waiting to be redeemed. Neither the celebration of Christmas nor the genius of Shakespeare truly recovers within time a timeless Eden, says Auden, whatever sentimentalists and the Romantic poets say.

Like the two ambitious works that have preceded it, *The Age of Anxiety* is dramatic in its form but not a stage play. The first part is not a sequence of spoken dialogue but one of thought; then the characters speak to each other, grow closer, and seem to function virtually as a single mind, so that the movement of the dreamlike play is from isolation to communal awareness. The subtitle for this elaborate drama is "A Baroque Eclogue." It is baroque, precisely, in its elaborate form, and an eclogue in that once more it contains tracts of poetry about the landscape—even though its literal setting is a bar in Manhattan, and in fantasy it moves from pastoral to urban.

There are four people in the cast: Quant, a middle-aged man whose very ordinary life and work make him seem, to himself, a failure, and who gazes at his reflection in the mirror as if it were another self, with other possibilities; Malin, a medical intelligence officer in the Canadian Air Force, who contemplates in his mirror the singular nature of the human animal with its self-consciousness; Rosetta, a successful buyer for a store but a lone and lonely, alienated woman; and Emble, a young American sailor, insecure and trying to establish his identity. All speak, and the verse of this work is largely written, in alliterative lines, with echoing sounds that are the aural equivalent of the mirror, sometimes a magic mirror and an opening to a dream world of psychic reality, like Alice's looking glass, yet also a distorting mirror. These four think, look, and hear. They hear the radio giving news of the war, to which each reacts in a passage of reflection. The passages end, one after the other, with the same refrain: "Many have perished; more will." It is evident already that their minds are coming closer, one to another.

Now they speak: Emble talks about the barbarism of the past, of uncivilized times, Malin of the barbarism still inherent in civilization, in the city, Quant asks what will come after this barbarous warfare, and Rosetta speaks about the weight of the cruel past upon the cursed future. Malin describes the condition of the "traveller through Time," always trapped in his Now, "not Being" what "he was willed to become." They realize that they are all such travelers, fellow travelers. They leave their bar stools and move together to a booth, where they continue to drink, think, dream, speak. This is the end of Part One.

With Part Two, "The Seven Ages," the reader begins to understand why the setting for the verse play is a bar on the eve of All Saints' Day, that is, Hallowe'en. As the alcohol they consume frees their fancies, they assume masks and guises, they are freed to remember and act out past times of life and to dream of the future. These times are versions in the mind of Shakespeare's "seven ages" of humanity. Each person then contemplates childhood with its fresh joys and pains; adolescence and its dreams; youth, loneliness, the frustrated need to love; adulthood, apparent solidity and hidden doubt, a need for assurance and for meaning, for a core of identity; middle age with its delusion of success but a continued doubt of purpose and a continual sense of being alone; later age and reveries that imagine an unreal past along with a hidden feeling of failure, of foolishness (at this point, the juke box plays a bawdy song on that abased and unstable creature the "Asterisk," "Approximate," "Transient," "Guttering," "Camouflage," "Watery" Man); and then old age and death, not a quest finding the goals, but journey's end. Now all four are, returning to their present selves, ready to set out on their quest, going beyond memory and anticipation in their attempt to imagine, through visions of landscape, a landscape representing the human body but also the stages in a soul's development. This will be a journey again, but not one through time.

Part Three, "The Seven Stages," presents that quest and brings in the familiar elements of the poet's imagination: the settings of mountain, watershed, valley, plain, city, wa-

ter, wilderness, their psychic and bodily equivalents, and
the theme of the fallen being who seeks Eden, or lost innocence. Each of the four speakers has a vision, and, now
drinking and half dreaming—for theirs is distinctly a landscape of dreams—each perceives and describes a part of her
and his route. They begin on the dull plain of the present,
perhaps suggesting Arnold's "darkling plain" and certainly
anticipating one of the *Bucolics*, "Plains," which describes
this as the most frustrating of geographical settings. Separately, they move into the mountains, which are menacing
but provide waterfalls of encouragement. Then, still singly,
all enter a valley, perhaps the valley of the shadow of death,
an echo of the twenty-third Psalm of David.

Entering that valley and then ascending a steep pass, they
arrive at a watershed—another favorite spot in Auden's
landscape—where they complete the first stage of the journey, and where, at a ramshackle tavern, the things in their
landscape seem familiar. One can guess now that the plains
may signify the feet or the pedestrian diurnal life, mountains the mind with its anxieties and hope, the valley and
the rocky pass going upward, the backbone, and the watershed, which is finally called "high heartland," the heart or
inmost feeling. The maritime flats to which they next de-
scend make up a border area, facing on the open sea, and it
suggests the face one has as well as the public face one puts
on. Malin senses at this point that the ocean is near; and
soon they arrive, "two and two," at "rival ports." These
may be the eyes that observe a world outside, the oceanic
nature of the environment. But here, as often, the parallels
of landscape with body are at best tenuous. From here they
travel on—Rosetta and Emble, the younger ones, by air-
plane, Malin and Quant, the older, by train. Nobody walks,
but the idea of propulsion, of movement, may suggest the
legs. In transport, they are surrounded by people of various
sorts with whose guilt, falsehood, and attractiveness they
must be associated, alternately despising and feeling drawn
to these others (as one may be on a noisy, crowded train,

plane, or subway). Their destination is the city, the place of
the crowd and of estrangement, of civilization and of incivi-
lilty; and when they arrive at the station there and at the
terminal, to meet up again, they greet one another: They
are united. All the parts of the landscape seem now to co-
here as the city represents the whole body. So it will do in
the later elegy on Yeats. The city is the social body, too, the
community here and now, lively and yet in danger of decay.
From this city they take a trolley going north into the suburbs, as though following the arms and hands to the far
fingers of the city. There they see a great house, to which
Rosetta—whose fantasies are all of life in British country
estates—rushes with enthusiasm, only to return in bitter
disappointment. The great house is a rectory where the
jaded rector, not at all someone out of Trollope or even
Agatha Christie, no longer believes in hell: This is a
"World that is fallen." The fourth stage of their travel ends
with that rueful thought, at this decayed house; and the
fifth begins and ends in a graveyard.

They proceed, Rosetta and Quant by canoe, Malin and
Emble on bicycles. And they arrive at a setting of Italian
gardens. If the graveyard has suggested a body in decay, the
gardens may suggest the hope for a body perfected, risen,
redeemed. But these are gardens, not the Garden; imitating
Eden, they must in this fallen time and place be also mazes,
where the lost wander.

When at last they emerge from their meandering paths,
they are nearing the end of the journey, the end of the seventh stage; they are in a wasteland. In fact, they are back
where they began, with dazed minds and infirm bodies, in
the bar at closing time. They have been dreaming. The end
of the quest, as always, is the self in time: self-under-
standing, which means an understanding of limitation and
of what cannot be found yet or held here, the timeless.

Delusion, doubt, a sense of universal riddle and individual ridiculousness remain. So Part Four is called "The
Dirge," to imply perhaps that the questers' hope is dead.

Yet, something important has happened, and all have had visions. This dirge includes an allusion to the harrowing of Hell, as a sign that the world of lost souls—and bodies— will be redeemed, for the Maker still sustains it. All four characters now take a cab to Rosetta's apartment, resolving at least to seem more cheerful.

In the apartment a strange party takes place, "The Masque," in which each person plays a role. Auden's recognition that every human being must act a part or parts and cannot be wholly sincere—the idea playfully spelled out in his poem "Many Happy Returns"—is evident here. They sing and they dance: Rosetta, transformed into a kind of Venus, in Emble's arms. What begins as play becomes playfulness, and then lovemaking. Malin and Quant leave Rosetta and Emble alone, but after she has seen them to the elevator and returns, she finds Emble passed out in the bedroom. In a long, lovely, and moving lyric, she reflects on his being like a bridegroom who overdid the wedding festivities and cannot perform nuptial duty; she also reflects that this might be in some way a matter of his knowing, as she knows, that they are not suited to each other. In part because that is so, she can regard him tenderly, lovingly. She concludes the masque with words in Hebrew—Rosetta is Jewish and, being of the ancient chosen people, represents the religious strain that underlies all this work—"Hear, O Israel, the Lord our God, the Lord is One." This is the basic and essential prayer of Judaism, spoken before sleep, before death, and this affirmation is appropriate not only to the time of night but also to this time in the masque, the play within the play. Above and beneath the cracks and crookedness, the mazes and the many, there is One.

In the "Epilogue," Malin and Quant exchange addresses and go their separate ways, Quant anticipating peace in this world now at war, and Malin making peace with himself, caring less about earthly failure or success. At least, Quant modifies his cynicism, and Malin tries to give up his self-pity. Malin concludes that each person belongs to all others in the common lot of humankind. The knowledge that these four have come to is negative—the quest has not arrived at the cross, at perfect clarity, or even common sense—but it is knowledge, and it allows this life to continue, even in the present age of anxiety. It is All Saints' Day, and in some small way each of these four has become one of God's holy people.

Auden's later dramatic work takes the form of operatic libretto. As early as 1941 he wrote one such script, *Paul Bunyan,* for the music of Benjamin Britten. This is a vaguely Brechtian folk opera in which the title character does not appear but is a voice speaking from the wings. The central actor on stage is Johnny Inkslinger, Bunyan's bookkeeper. The piece includes a good deal of political satire, but its main theme is the taming of the wilderness, a work which, being accomplished, allows the main characters to move on to New York and Hollywood. Regarded as something of a failure by audience, author, and composer—it ran for a week in Brander Matthews Hall at Columbia University—it was never published and is not available except as a much-amended manuscript in the Columbia library.

In 1947, Igor Stravinsky asked Auden to provide a libretto based on the Hogarth series of prints, "The Rake's Progress." The result was an Auden-Kallman collaborative effort, in which the composer himself took part during the outlining of the scenario. *The Rake's Progress,* subtitled simply "A Fable," uses now familiar elements, the theme of a pastoral lost Eden, the tale of Venus and Adonis, the Faust legend. Anne Trulove and Tom Rakewell, the rake-to-be, are at the beginning innocent young lovers in Maytime. But Tom, unwilling to work, trusts too much in his wish for fortune. When he dreams of having unearned money, the satanic figure of Nick Shadow appears to announce that Tom has inherited a fortune. There is a price to be paid for the legacy: Nick shadows Tom from now on, taking him to London and, in the second scene, to Mother

Goose's house of prostitution. Here the lust of Venus and Mars is reenacted, as the young man, no longer so innocent, is urged to "follow Nature," his own flawed and fallen nature. In a third scene Anne follows Tom to the city, to find and perhaps yet to rescue Tom.

Act Two reveals the young man already jaded, bored by nature and unhappy with his own nature. He does not believe himself free, as he had thought to be. Nick persuades him to marry Baba, the bearded Turkish lady, proving his freedom, just because there is no reason to make such an odd alliance. One is reminded of Gide's *Les Caves du Vatican,* in which the protagonist tries to prove his total triumph over necessity, or causality, by committing an irrational murder; it is the *"acte gratuit,"* and it proves self-defeating because it is after all motivated by a proud person's desire not to be motivated. By trying to demonstrate his freedom, Tom has demonstrated that he is imprisoned. Anne appears, and Tom bitterly regrets his foolish marriage. The ludicrous Baba chatters and sings a patter song; Tom silences her, but remains discontented. At last, he sleeps and dreams of a machine that can turn stones into bread. When he awakens, and wishes that the dream were true, Nick makes it so by producing the very machine. This section apparently amounts to an inversion of Matthew 7:9, "What man is there of you, whom if his son ask bread, will he give him a stone?" Tom believes that the marvelous machine will abolish hunger, bring Eden back again, and somehow once more win his Anne for him. But Nick Shadow, confidence man, has given him only an illusion; Tom asks for bread, and Nick indeed gives him what is only a stone.

In the third act, Tom is ruined and must sell everything. Even Baba is up for auction. She tells Anne that she will return to the stage and leave Tom to his true love. But it is too late. Tom attempts suicide, only to have time stopped by Nick as he is about to kill himself. Nick offers him another chance. He has only to name three playing cards correctly. Again, Nick cheats and Tom seems about to lose the game—for Nick has used the same card, the hellish Queen of hearts, twice. But, unpredictably, Tom chooses right, and the Mephistophelian Nick is foiled. In revenge, Nick makes Tom mad; and the damaged hero ends his life in Bedlam, the mental hospital, dreaming that he is Adonis and that Anne has come to him as Venus. She is the Queen of Hearts that he has chosen, not now Queen of Hell but beatific vision.

The epilogue gives the moral that the Devil finds work for idle hands. It may seem a too simple conclusion for this Christian and antiexistentialist work, but it stresses the cental ideas of human beings' needing to work, choose, and finally accept. Tom's final act was a labor of faith, a choice of love.

The opera was first performed (1951) in Venice, at Teatro La Fenice, to considerable acclaim. The Metropolitan Opera produced it in New York in 1953, with much less success. Auden intensely disliked the New York performance, saying that the singers were all wrong except Mack Harrell, whom he very much admired. The others, he maintained, both sang and acted badly. It was not produced again by the Metropolitan. In printed form (it was first published in 1951) it has remained a major and a widely admired part of the Auden canon, and it is probably the best example of Auden's and Kallman's collaboration.

The two worked together again to write *Delia, or A Masque of Night*, a "Libretto for a one-act opera," and this shorter work was not set to music, nor did it appear upon the stage. It is based on George Peele's play *The Old Wives' Tale*, but neither plot nor language follows Peele closely. The fantastic nature of the piece, which combines heroic romance with elements of the fairy tale, is suggested by the characters' names: Orlando, the knight who undertakes a quest to find the mysterious Delia of whom he has dreamed; the sorcerer Sacrapant, who holds her captive; the sorcerer's apprentice Bungay, who is turned into a bear, and his wife Xantippe, named appropriately after the shrew who was Socrates' mate and scold; and a series of allegorical figures called Time, Mutability, Toil, Age, Death, and Pain, who appear in a pageant. The effect is at once fanciful and highly serious. The script incorporates familiar myth and folklore: When Orlando breaks a vow by drawing his sword to defend his Delia, he seems to have lost her forever, but an old crone, who has already given him the magic willow twig that allows him to find his beloved, now offers to liberate the captive if Orlando will marry her, the crone herself, and thus give up his Delia. To save Delia, Orlando agrees. Now, as always in the versions of this old tale, the ugly crone is revealed as something quite different. She is really the Queen of the Night (an echo of Mozart) and is sometimes called Diana, sometimes Dame Nature—one of Auden's favorite terms—or simply the original Mother. In fact, she evokes the image of Robert Graves's White Goddess, the primal being of the sort referred to by Goethe in *Faust* as the fearful "Mothers."[5] There is even an element of *Macbeth* in this tale; Sacrapant feels safe because of a prophecy that only one born "motherless" can overcome him; but Orlando, aided by this natural Mother figure, has literally been so born, for his mother died just before his birth. Heroism and the mythic powers triumph at last, and dark magic is defeated: Those men who have been transformed into animals are returned to their own forms, and a loyal Orlando is joined with his chastened Delia.

Delia was not set to music, but its manner is wholly lyric and thus musical. It remains a charming part of the Auden (and Kallman) canon.

The *Elegy for Young Lovers* was set to music; it was written for the German composer Hans Werner Henze, and again it is a work of collaboration, the libretto being done by Auden and Kallman once more. The action is set in the Austrian Alps. The central character is a poet who believes, it appears, those lines of Yeats that declare that a man, specifically an artist, must choose between "Perfection of the life or of the work." Mittenhofer, the Viennese poet, chooses the work and is willing to sacrifice his own integrity and the lives of others to perfect his work. He uses other people and their experiences as the raw material for his verse: in particular, the aging and deranged Hilda Mack's memory of her bridegroom's death forty years ago, and her visions—including the vision of Mittenhofer's mistress Elizabeth and the son of his doctor, young Toni, holding hands in an "Eden" that is snowbound. The other characters, including the doctor and the poet's secretary Carolina, see Mittenhofer in various ways and sing of his tyranny and his genius. The body of Hilda's dead husband is discovered in a glacier. He is the bridegroom of the past. Toni, in love with Elizabeth, who replaces his dead mother just as Mittenhofer is Elizabeth's substitute for her father, hopes to be the bridegroom of the future. This is "The Emergence of the Bridegroom," to be succeeded by "The Emergence of the Bride," the second act. Now Elizabeth must choose whether to fulfill herself as woman and wife by accepting Toni or to be the muse of great poetry by remaining with Mittenhofer. She accepts Toni, and they are married.

The third act, then, is "Man and Wife." The marriage is of short duration. The old poet does not warn the two young lovers of an impending blizzard but sends them out into the mountains, where on their wedding night they die in their cold Eden. The work ends with Mittenhofer reciting his elegy for them, the poem that their being sacrificed has allowed him to complete. The poet triumphant is clearly revealed as supreme Romantic egoist.

The *Elegy* is the most psychologically complex and in many ways the most verbally intricate of the dramatic pieces at which Auden labored. It reveals not only the "guilt of the artist" but a specific and personal fear that he increasingly felt of allowing himself to concentrate upon artistry rather than honesty, poetic effects rather than people.

In some sense, virtually all Auden's work in the dramatic form can be called religious. To some extent, each work opposes Romantic art to Christian art, self-absorption to the recognition of otherness, of sacredness, of mystery. He is not often thought of or written of as a dramatist, and his plays and libretti are likely to include a good many purely lyric passages. Yet, from the earliest part of his career, he was drawn to the dramatic mode.[6] It is, for him, a means of expressing the need for dialogue, of the interrelating of persons, that is a moral imperative, whether its languge is political, psychological, or sacramental. Auden is a poet of the community, the communion of people.

4

Prose

Just as the plays are largely in verse and include lyric passages, some of which the author excerpted and published separately in volumes of his poetry, so what is called here Auden's prose work, work of literary and social criticism or comment, often has poetic qualities and sometimes includes poetic passages. This is true of his first volume in prose, *The Orators,* which appeared in 1932.

The Orators has generally been regarded as his most obscure attempt at expository writing; in fact, it is perhaps less expository than didactic, and a good many readers may well wonder what it is trying to teach. It is, in any event, about teaching; apparently the title refers to the teacher in the classroom, and Auden was a schoolmaster during this period, the early thirties. From his own comments and those of others, he does not appear to have been very oratorical in his classroom, preferring to surprise, amuse, and gain response from his students. Still, the position of a master is rather like that of the speaker on a platform, especially from the student's point of view; and it is the student's point of view with which this work begins, encapsulated in lively if ambiguous verse.

That verse prologue, reprinted later under the title "Adolescence," describes the young man, or boy becoming man, as he wanders over mountain, pasture, grove, determined to be honest and brave—only to return home from war and be condemned as coward and deceiver. The blithe and at the same time deeply anxious mood of the adolescent is caught here, in the introduction to a work on just how crucial to a man's life the formative boyhood years in school invariably are. Now, the points of view will alternate: that of the troubled and ambivalent boy— ambivalent about adult authority and about his own ability, his courage, his sexuality—and that of the politically radical master who is nevertheless part of a very conventional hierarchy.

The hierarch is satirized with the parodic language of Book I, "The Initiates." There are four academic orators represented here, the first one a version—according to Isherwood—of the headmaster of St. Edmund's, the school where both Auden and Isherwood were students.[1] Yet in this rather ponderous section there is a moral point: The perversion, exaggeration, or failure of love brings about psychic and physical illness. That is at least in part the point of the "Address for a Prize-Day." The next oration, or "Argument," has to do with the need for heroism, the quest both seemingly necessary and essentially foolish for a secular Messiah. Its second section prays to every possible and impossible source for deliverance; its third section concludes with the priest's words in the graveyard being blown away by the wind. Then, a "Statement" deals with the evolution of humankind toward some new and better life.[2] All these schoolmasterly pronouncements, however, are too simple and too pompous. The fourth, most memorable, and perhaps most serious part of this first book is the "Letter to a Wound." That narrative reflection and address is a remarkable revelation of how being wounded, ill, can result from spiritual faults and yet reconcile a person to failures or to any facile view of life; the writer addresses his own wound with love, for in maturity he has come to cherish it. If there is perplexing uncertainty of tone throughout this prose, the ambiguity of it all is strongest and, strangely, most effective here. Is the letter writer morbid, or self-destructively neurotic? Is he a person strong enough to accept and even take pleasure in his interesting condition, his unavoidable condition? He seems to be both at once. The section ends, "Better burn this."

Book II, "Journal of an Airman," introduces the writer's love of games, puzzles, diagrams. The airman, as Monroe Spears suggests, is probably to be taken as a grown-up schoolboy, still in part protesting—and still, in part, rightly so—against adult tyranny, in the form of capitalist exploitation but also of any single, simple application of harsh rules.[3] His awareness of "the enemy," embodying that organized and disorganizing tyranny, is first given in a curious test: If, from an intersected figure, someone chooses to make either of two symmetrical crosses, the person is a friend, but anyone who chooses instead an irregular form is the enemy, to be shot at once. The use of this and other visual plans, the apparently mad leaping from maxim to metaphor, from alphabet to calendar, make this long, apparently ordered but meandering, dreamlike section especially difficult to follow. Its sense seems to be that the young man's life is a contest, a journey, a preparation for possible warfare, a quest for conquest of the enemy without and within the self.

The last parts of *The Orators* are entirely in verse: "Six Odes," addressed to the self, as well as Spender and Isherwood, to Gabriel Carritt of Sedbergh School, Edward Upward, "Schoolmaster," John Warner, Auden's pupils; the sixth one, somewhat oddly, is a petition, perhaps a prayer for a school chapel. The theme of education, using the figures of master and student, is maintained to the end.

The Epilogue is the part of this whole work that is best known, the often-anthologized lines beginning "O where are you going? said reader to rider." Using a version of Anglo-Saxon alliteration with medial caesuras strong enough to suggest half-line division, it emphasizes finally the need to overcome adolescence's paralyzing anxiety about the dangers in the world and the weaknesses in oneself, the need to travel, choose—to act. The truly adult human being is a rider, farer, hearer—and doer.

Auden later wrote of *The Orators* that it had a good idea which his "incompetence or impatience prevented from coming to much." He thought it too labored, too obscure. Yet it remains an intriguing puzzle and it did produce in the very last lines of verse some splendid work, a small triumph of poetry derived as it were from a great mass of prose.

From the fairly early thirties until the end of the decade, Auden was writing reviews and occasional articles for British and, later, American journals. He reviewed books on literary subjects, but also memoirs, popular works on science, and education. Often such reviews provided vehicles for the exposition of his own ideas on all these matters. Commenting on E. E. Phare's study of Hopkins, for instance, he wrote of a poet's need to observe reticence especially in matters of sex and religion (he thought that Hopkins's verse was sometimes marred by that poet's trying but being unable to disguise his homosexual feelings).[4] The articles touch on a great range of topics, including group living and the middle class, psychology and art, poetry and the film, philosophies and morality, the poetry of John Skelton and of Pope.[5] He edited anthologies, *The Poet's Tongue* (with John Garrett) in 1935 and *The Oxford Book of Light Verse* in 1938. In 1936 his selection of poetry by Robert Frost had been published with a critical introduction, in which was made clear—as a reading of his very earliest unpublished poetry reveals—the important influence that the American poet had upon him.

Auden's and MacNeice's *Letters from Iceland* (1937) is another volume that combines poetry and prose. It begins with the first part of a verse epistle to Byron, in the form and style of *Don Juan,* and the essays and letters that follow, some apparently actual letters and some to fictional persons, make up a miscellany of information about Iceland and comment on friendship, love, and politics. There is really no attempt to make this a perfectly coherent whole; but the collection is full of wit, variety, high seriousness, and mere playfulness, and it is almost always interesting; it is sometimes impressive. The five-part letter to Lord Byron that punctuates the work, serving as parts I, V, VIII, XII, and XVI, uses Byronic satire for contemporary comment, giving something of a framework to the varied whole—some parts of which are by MacNeice alone, although the last part, a final will and testament, is by both authors.

After all this comes an epilogue in verse which again combines commentary on the larger world of this dark moment with a tribute to what Auden thought of as his ancestral home. The fall of Seville seems here to be a danger signal, a sign of the worldwide conflict now threatening humankind. This is a last toast before the "gun-butt" strikes at the door. Soon, then, that ancestral island home will have to be left behind, that place that is in some way a make-believe Eden.

Yet Iceland is a real here-and-now place, and both Auden and MacNeice are poets of reality. One supposes that the appendix was Auden's idea to begin with: It includes graphs indicating land area, urbanized area, and the extent of the nation's foreign trade. Finally, there is a map of the country. Auden loved graphs and charts, and above all, maps; this appendix appears, then, to be a characteristic touch and an appropriate final document.

Auden contributed to another travel book, or again a travel book of sorts, this time collaborating with Isherwood on *Journey to a War*, an account of their experiences in Spain but also a political and poetic response to the darkening skies of Europe. Isherwood's prose report is like a cry of despair. Virtually all that Auden contributed to this volume, however, is verse—including his "In Time of War," a series of sonnets with a commentary.

Journey to a War was published in 1939. Auden wrote no more travel books of any sort, in poetry or prose. During the forties, he produced a number of reviews and articles—more reviews than essays, although he did pieces on "Criticism in a Mass Society," "The Role of Intellectuals in Political Affairs," "A Note on Order" (an interesting comment upon order both political and artistic, for *The Nation*), and an introduction to Isherwood's translation of Baudelaire's journals, as well as an introduction to James's *The American Scene*, and a lively introduction to the *Portable Greek Reader*, which he edited for the Viking Press. His critical prose was intended to be occasional, and when he collected it in *The Dyer's Hand*, he did so reluctantly, did it, as he said, only for the money.

In the meantime, he was lecturing, and some of his lectures were too significant not to be printed. At the University of Virginia, he gave a series of three such talks, dense and demanding, which were published in 1950 under the title *The Enchafèd Flood: The Romantic Iconography of the Sea*. It makes one of the most brilliant critiques of the Romantic mind and of Romantic poetry ever written.

This work is especially brilliant on Wordsworth, that poet whom the younger Auden had disdained. Even now, his response to Wordsworth is ambivalent. He interprets the dream in Book V of *The Prelude*, in which a strange figure carrying a stone and a shell appears to the dreamer, to guide him through a desert, by asserting that the stone is exact knowledge and the echoing shell is vatic knowledge, both poetic and prophetic. Beyond this desert is the city, the order of civilization that requires both kinds of knowledge—something of what C. P. Snow will call "the Two Cultures." Yet Wordsworth, and every Romantic mind, looks backward to and longs for the ocean and the desert, not forward to the city, which now seems decayed, corrupt. And for Auden the idea of the Just City, even though imperfectly realized in a fallen here and now, is an imperative. Civilization is as necessary as it is, in part at least, illusory. And those workmen and artists who try to repair it are more responsible than the enticing Romantics.

The unheroic City of Man, containing a society and cultivating, ordering, external nature, is still a shadow somehow of the City of God. The appeal of Romanticism is its celebration of the primal elements, first of all the sea and then the uncultivated desert which it imagines as a garden, as The Garden, Eden heroically achieved through a return to innocence. The Romantic artist at his most intense has a vision of apotheosis, an immanent divinity; and this means denying the obviously artificial restraints of urban life. So Auden explicates the Romantic poet's glorying in that ocean which in ancient times, for voyagers, was a place of danger—as the desert, for nomads, was a place of aridity— and he explains the Romantic emphasis upon the primacy of childhood, the sacredness of early memories.

Yet, finally, it is not by those Romantic illusions that the post-Romantic mind is threatened. As Eliot writes in "Prufrock" about the Romantic dream of mermaids, "human voices wake us, and we drown." The danger now seems to be that civilized post-Romantic and indeed postmodern people will be seduced by other illusions, by the False City of tyranny. It is clear at last that Auden in these brilliant lectures can perceive the validity as well as the impossibility of a Romantic iconography, the strength of Wordsworth's responses to civilization as well as its delusive appeal: It is as true that fallible human beings can be betrayed by a vicious and manipulative show of order, a "New Order," as that they have been likely to dream of a return on earth to the original, natural order which is only the chaos of sea and desert. Civilization is an ideal tenuous and fragile.

The Enchafèd Flood puzzled most of its auditors and many of its readers. It is not altogether easy reading. It is, however, Auden's greatest achievement in straightforward prose that brings together literary, social, moral, and religious criticism.

Throughout the next decade, he was producing reviews and essays for periodicals, a good many of them to be collected in *The Dyer's Hand*, in 1962. That volume, although it lacks a single unifying theme, represents something of the richness of his mind and pen in a period of great intellectual productivity. It is perhaps the one collection of his prose that remains best known. The book is dedicated to his Oxford tutor Nevill Coghill, with thanks for a home filled with books, a childhood in the country, and this tutor in whom he could confide. It might be called a "retrospective." Amusingly, in the Foreword the author comments that he has written poetry out of love, but prose upon demand—for a lecture, or an introduction, or a review. The effect might seem to be a diminishing of the importance of these pieces. For a good many readers, however, Auden remains one of the most compelling critical voices of his era.

The volume commences with a number of aphorisms under the titles "Reading" and "Writing." In the midst of comments on readers and writers, on the difference between critic and poet, there is a curious section about "Eden," its language, landscape, architecture, and so on. This is Auden at play, mapping out his own ideal place. The climate is British, the formal dress French (in the style of the 1830s and 1840s), the economic activities mining and farming, and there are no cars or airplanes, no movies, radio, or television. The observations on writing and writers are sharp and often delightfully fanciful, and they include an especially interesting statement that it is impossible to define the difference between poetry and prose.

What appears to be the first true essay in this volume was in fact, to begin with, a lecture, the inaugural lecture that Auden delivered as professor of poetry at Oxford. It is called "Making, Knowing and Judging," and it is concerned with the poet, the scholar, and the critic. The speaker's predecessors in the Oxford chair, including Matthew Arnold, had sometimes represented all these functions, as surely Auden himself does. Scholar he is, not so much in the American academic sense of researcher as in the older one, still to be assumed in Britain, of a person versed in language and literature. The piece begins with and inevitably returns to the role of the poet and of poetry. Interestingly, the printed version of this address, given at one of the ancient English universities, has as its epigraph a sentence from the American writer Thoreau, who might perhaps be called by none of those titles—poet, scholar, critic. But the quotation is about the poet: "The art of life, of a poet's life, is, not having anything to do, to do something." Does this imply that poetry is wholly autonomous (after all, Auden has written that it "makes nothing happen")? No, not for Auden, not ever. After sustained discourse on the discipline, on the need for poets as for scholars and critics to be ordered and honest, the piece ends by declaring that whatever else it does, whether it delights, amuses, or instructs, the poet's art must praise, must praise for "being and for happening." It sounds like an echo of the elegy on Yeats, with its memorable words, "Teach the free man how to praise." And it reminds us, as the sense of this lecture-essay woud suggest, that although poetry is not religion or its surrogate, as Matthew Arnold would have it, it is in a sense religious.

In "The Virgin and the Dynamo," Auden echoes and alters the terms used by Henry Adams, asserting that Adams confused the Virgin of Chartres with Venus, who is in fact—being a pagan mythic figure identified with physical nature—the Dynamo "in disguise." Auden's Dynamo is the speechless natural world, contrasted to the historical world of the Virgin, which can be described only by speech (as the Word is uttered and history given meaning, along with the possibility of historical time's being redeemed, by the Virgin Mother). Both the natural and the historical are real worlds, made up of a number of beings. That number can be described as a Crowd, a mere mass; or a Society, a group of related beings held together in a system; or a Community, a body of members united by a common devotion to something other than the self. The dynamic natural world has only societies, whereas the historical world—"worded" by the Virgin, to use a term from Hopkins—can comprise communities. The essay proceeds to define the human being as at once a natural, an individual, body and mind and a historical soul and spirit, an ordered and ordering or morally active creature. Finally, poets combine all these elements, for a true poem unifies natural society and historic community, the outside and the human or inward orders; the implication seems to be at last that even the best poetry, attempting an analogy to the perfect ordering of Eden, is imperfect, for it is contained within imperfect, disorderly time, within history. The logic of this piece requires close reading to follow, but it becomes apparent that Auden is moving from Henry Adams's distinction between a historic religious society and the twentieth-century world of science and technology to a revised idea of religious history and natural phenomena which are to be brought together by the poet. Auden, after all, has accommodated in his poetry the Christmas story and a celebration of landscapes, mines, machineries. In a sense, then, the essay can be read as an explanation of his own intent and practice.

Again, in "The Poet and the City," the critic comments upon his own poetic themes, the nature of poetic art and the need for, but the failures of, civilization. This is less a carefully developed essay, however, than a series of observations, even epigrams and aperçus. The author is concerned with what it is to be a poet and with the dangers to the poet of living in the city, of becoming a public person—as well as the poet's need, certainly Auden's own need, for urban life. If, in spite of his own refusal to be a political poet after his early attempts, he recognizes here that the making of a poem is a political act, he believes that he must assume and then ignore that truth. He has to remember that, although he should tell each truth as best he can, the artist is always at play, asserting the essential human "right to frivolity." This is the third of the three pieces in Part II, "The Dyer's Hand," each, in its way, about how the writer adopts to, is colored by, what he writes about, frivolous or solemn.

The next piece in this collection, "Hic et Ille"—here or this and there or that—may be an echo of Yeats, for Auden, like Yeats, posits two versions of one identity. This, however, is a moral piece, as Yeats's is not, and it distinguishes

Ego from Self. Ego is the sense, illusory but pervasive, of one's own unchanging reality, a sense represented by the distorting mirror that each person carries in the mind. The classic figure of Ego is Narcissus gazing at himself in the pool, not with desire but with rapt contemplation, while Echo languishes—and this rather bawdy passage has Narcissus preferring his pistol to his penis, fancying that he can control one, not the other.[6] "The Well of Narcissus" is the title for the third section of the book, in which this is the first of four pieces. The later literary representation is Don Quixote, with his illusions about who he is. Ego can feel shame but not guilt, even as he is guilty of the greatest sin, the basic human trait of pride. Self is not the idea but the physical and mental fact of a changing "me." It is represented by Sancho Panza, it can feel guilt, and it is guilty of vanity and all the other sins of body and mind that are smaller, less heroic, than Lucifer's pride. Self is ordinary and has a history. The four parts of this essay are A, B, C, D; Ego is A, Self is B. C is the physical nature which is primary for selfhood, and D, the spiritual or emotional which dominates in the Egoist. The extremes of Egoism (elsewhere Auden might well call it Romantic Egoism) and of independent Selfhood are two forms of madness. A, Ego, may be deluded by thinking either "I am God" or "I am a devil," while B, Self, may vainly suppose "I am free" or "I am only a thing." Finally, A's God is Zeus or the Almighty with whom one identifies or against whom one rebels, but B's God is the "Unmoved Mover," unconstraining or indifferent. Although all this moral and psychological discourse is directly relevant to Auden's poetry, "Hic et Ille" is not quite literary criticism. The reader might well suppose, rather, that he is writing in generally valid terms about his ego and self, although not only about himself.

Among Auden's efforts in prose, "Balaam and His Ass" was one of his own favorites. It combines criticism with moral commentary and an essentially religious conclusion; it can be taken as an extended footnote to his poetry. In all, this is a long, dazzling, often confusing and often illuminating sequence of remarks on Ego and Self again (but with further complications), on *The Tempest* and *Don Quixote* again, on *King Lear*, on Goethe's *Faust*, Mozart's *Don Giovanni* (apparently Auden's favorite opera), and Wagner's *Tristan und Isolde*, as well as Jules Verne and P. G. Wodehouse. It begins with a definition of the master-servant relationship. That relationship is a dialogue that is social, historical, and contractual, for a servant—Quixote's Sancho Panza and Pickwick's Sam Weller reveal this—is a free agent, not a slave. This dialogue is apparently the basis for the thou-to-thou social intercourse which distinguishes but relates persons in great art. *Thou* is used instead of *you* not only for the biblical overtone of the Authorized Version, but also to avoid the ambiguity of contemporary English by which one cannot distinguish *you* meaning one person from a general form of address; and the dialogue here is between one and one other. There are now various forms of Ego, the cognitive, the volitional (which cannot be a master), and the Superego of Freud, which masters, controls, cautions—and may or may not be obeyed by the self. The willing or volitional Ego, which appears to be the Ego of "Hic et Ille," is free of demands from others and yet longs to be loved by another, in order to have its own being validated: This is the condition of the proud and fallen being. After a series of brilliant critical forays in which these terms are applied to great poetic works, the essay ends by invoking Wodehouse's wise servant Jeeves, who is like the talking ass in the Book of Numbers, the beggar who advises the hero on his quest, the comic and clever servant (and great Christian art, Auden suggests, is comedy, not tragedy), and who speaks in the voice of "Agape, of holy love."

Auden could perceive the comic element in art of the highest seriousness and the serious element in entertainments apparently frivolous. A friend of Edmund Wilson's, he could not agree with that quite humorless (if impressive) critic's querulous outburst, "Who Cares Who Killed Roger

Ackroyd?" "The Guilty Vicarage" is about detective stories, to which Auden was addicted, as are those, in general,
who love verbal games and puzzles. The older critic's dis-
dain for that genre revealed, for Auden, why Wilson might
be an intellectual but could never be a poet. This did not
and does not mean that Auden regards detective stories as
works of art, although he asserts that an analysis of the
form can serve to help one understand the function of literary art. The mystery tale involves a dialogue between innocence and guilt, and, although it is distinctly not a form of
tragedy, it follows Aristotle's outline of the tragic plot,
from initial peace to mystery and the question of guilt, to
resolution after a period of suspense, to the final peace of
catharsis.

The difference is that in Greek tragedy the audience
knows the truth (suspense is illusory), whereas in the mystery tale the reader does not. In most good detective stories
there are elements of the Eden myth—but it can only be an
illusory Eden, the pleasant vicarage or country house—and
of the Quest. It is all fantasy, a pleasant game as well as a
cathartic relief to actual anxieties about violence and evil in
this world, and it takes place in a closed society that finally,
with the solution, is restored to its normal and Edenic state.
The fantasy of the story's reader is that of returning to the
Garden; and even though great works of literary art do not
at last indulge this fantasy, it is one with which they are
constantly and seriously concerned.

Auden intensely admired Kafka, and his short piece on
Kafka, "The I Without a Self," takes the life and work of a
great writer to be another quest, an inevitably frustrated
quest for identity, and, at the same time, an acknowledgment that our customary ideas of what is real cannot be
true conceptions of the ultimately real. Once more the no-
tions of the double self seeking an integrated identity, of the
search that is heroic and doomed, of the artist's painful
knowledge of exile from Eden, recur in Auden's critical
commentary.

Part IV of the collection is entitled "The Shakespearean City." Except for two interludes and a very brief postscript, the (seven) essays here are about Shakespeare, and, as is the case so often in Auden's prose as well as in his poetry, the critical rhetoric is based on the idea of *civitas*, the city, civilization, and its disruptions as well as its discontents. Shakespeare himself is seen as ambivalent, not as a distinctly Christian dramatist in the great tragedies, but not, either, a creator of truly tragic figures.

The relationship of Sophocles to Shakespeare is one of contrast. As the first essay observes, Elizabethans could have known very little of Greek drama, and they did—notably Shakespeare did—inherit elements from the medieval mystery plays that emerged from the church. Once more, the problem for Auden is that a Christian world cannot produce tragedy in the classical sense of the term. Shakespeare's tragic plays, he argues, are verbally magnificent presentations of crime or pathology, but their central heroes, if stripped naked of the rhetoric, appear as muddled, fallen, even foolish figures, not as noble tragic protagonists, whereas his comedies show real people in a real world. The idea may seem startling, but it is based on the Christian understanding that all human beings are fallible, foolish, potentially funny, and that no human being can be altogether noble in failure or suffering. In classical comedy, the butt of the joke lacks human dignity and can be simply laughed at; in Christian comedy, the buffoon is everyman. This is the central pont of "The Globe," Auden's first Shakespearean essay, and it is summed up at the end of this piece: A dramatic character for whom the author had either "absolute reverence" or "absolute contempt" would not be actable at the Globe or any later theatre.

"The Prince's Dog" is about Falstaff, who is compared, in a surprising conjunction that is characteristic of Auden, with Tristan and Don Giovanni, all persons without a past, without a childhood history. Once, we were all like Falstaff, selves lacking a superego, and the fact makes us respond to that curiously innocent rogue with affection. He is like the Sinner of Lublin whose radiance and very lack of repentance overwhelm the wise rabbi. Like Christ, finally, Falstaff can be regarded by a more worldly wisdom as a blasphemer and a bad companion. For Auden, the unregenerate Falstaff is a distinctly Christian comic being.

After an "Interlude: The Wish Game," with lively discourse on fairy tales, this section returns to Shakespeare in "Brothers and Others," on *The Merchant of Venice*. Now the essayist is concerned again with matters that appear or are implicit in his poetry and plays: the importance of the other, who should be respected and cherished for otherness, but usually is not; the historic relations of Christian and Jew; the danger of corruption in a city that is governed by commerce rather than commonality. Venice is a society of merchants, people who would be despised in the England of Henry IV; Portia's Belmont seems a fairy-tale place, but it is not a true Eden or even an honest country home deriving its beauty from agricultural abundance. Belmont wants to believe that people are good or bad by nature, Gentiles, who, like Bassanio, can stand "surety" for a brother-figure (although doing that is condemned by theologians as false pride) or Jews, who practice usury. But in the commercial Venice of this play, already, it is clear that people are interdependent, so that everyone is both really other and yet to be accepted as brother. As the final verse, quoted from Charles Williams, indicates, money and commercial exchange are not inherently evil, but the exchange must mean a communication between persons, a transaction of which neither Shylock nor Antonio is capable. So *The Merchant of Venice*, although posing serious problems, is one of Shakespeare's "Unpleasant Plays."

The next "Interlude" is entitled "West's Disease," and it is about the novels of Nathanael West, whose major characters, Auden asserts, suffer from the wish—it cannot, actually, be a desire—to be other than oneself. They pity others because they pity themselves, but pity is not compassion for it is arid and self-centered. West frighteningly reveals the symptoms of infection in a democratic and mechanized social order, the infection of despair.

The negativism of West's characters may find a counterpart in that of Iago, according to the next Shakespearean essay, "The Joker in the Pack." Iago as practical joker is the man who wishes to destroy for the sake of destroying, and that means destroying himself as well as others. The others are not let off lightly: Roderigo is neurotically uncertain of his own place, his own sexuality; Cassio is merely timid; Desdemona is drawn to Othello's glamour more than to himself and is proud of her power over him; Othello, finally, as a black man and an outsider in Venice, for all his military prowess upon which Venice must rely, has a hidden weakness, a desperate insecurity, because like Shylock he is for the proper Venetians an "other." For this and the earlier essay Venice is "The Shakespearean City," and it is no city of brotherly love. All can be victims of the tricks, the search for knowledge and not truth, the impartial malice that is the hating and self-hating of Iago, practical joker, manipulator, mad scientist.

The "Postscript" is upon "Infernal Science," the hellish pursuit of knowledge that would go beyond what can be known, the need to know absolutely, to reduce approximates to exacts. Behaviorist or deviser of bombs, the indifferent scientist is today's Iago.

Part Five of this collection, "Two Bestiaries," is on D. H. Lawrence and Marianne Moore as poets, the first a writer with whose ideas Auden largely disagreed and yet, for him, an honest, and often a tellingly satirical poet whom he could admire in part for being so different from Auden himself; the second, a poet whose work at first perplexed and then delighted him by its technical skill, exact observation, and delicacy, a poet who became his friend and of whom he could say that her verse convinces the reader of her being "personally good." These are fine and sensitive appreciations.

"The American Scene" comprises a group of brief critical studies, of Henry James's book with just that title, of Anzia Yezierska's autobiography (for the scene ranges from social life in Saratoga and Newport to the lives of immigrants in New York's Lower East Side), of Robert Frost's poetry (Frost, unlike Hopkins or Lawrence, has reticence, an "auditory chastity"), and then "American Poetry" in general. In these pieces Auden combines the nonnative's distanced view with the longtime resident's—and citizen's—involvement.

The extraordinary, sometimes dazzling, expanse of literary landscape that Auden can survey is nowhere more apparent than in Part Seven, "The Shield of Perseus." The somewhat cryptic title of this section refers to that shield on which the hero Perseus kept his gaze, seeing the deadly Gorgons only in its reflection so that their direct look would not slay him. Apparently the point is that a critic can deal with the most serious, perhaps dangerous matters—the danger being pomposity and earnest falsehood—by perceiving them in reflections that are comic, operatic, dramatic, seemingly frivolous. The Postscript is indeed in earnest: It is another comment upon "Christianity and Art." The method in the essays is in some ways indirect, seemingly tangential if not devious.

"Notes on the Comic" is an analytic exercise that uses instances from *Twelfth Night, Der Rosenkavalier, Charley's Aunt,* literary parody, and satire. Next comes a critique of Byron's *Don Juan,* which shows how Byron makes the reader giggle, not laugh, by his intrusion of the profane upon the sacred, in his loose and rapid, usually precise, and almost always comic, work. Byron represents the great comic poet, whose comedy retains for Auden serious implications. In "Dingley Dell and the Fleet," the critic returns to the idea of Eden, the attempt to recover the lost perfect place, an attempt that itself can be funny; and his points are made through analysis of *The Pickwick Papers,* moving from pastoral spot to prison, where funny old Mr. Pickwick can realize that—in debtor's prison—he *is* a debtor, but also one with kingly advantages that the illusory garden spot of Dingle Dell did not provide. The "Postscript," "The Frivolous and the Earnest." sums up the religious sense of all these essays upon comic themes. The author concludes that his duty to God is to be happy, his duty to his neighbor is to lessen pain and to give pleasure. This is what comedy does, fulfilling its sacred function. "Genius & Apostle" seems not to be about the comic at all: It comprises critical comments on two plays by Ibsen, a satirical genius, on Don Quixote as a version of the Christian Knight-Errant, an apostle. Again, there are in fact serious wit and earnest comedy in these works. Finally, the ultimate Postscript, "Christianity and Art," is an almost casual brief summation. Here Auden recognizes that there cannot be a Christian culture (surely this observation implies disagreement with Eliot and his idea of an actually impossible "Christian Society"), and that Christian art often cannot be overt (once more, he notes that some intensely personal religious poems by Donne and Hopkins make him uneasy). The duty of the Christian artist is to please and bless God and his neighbor by making the best thing possible.

The final section of *The Dyer's Hand* reveals Auden in other hues, reminding us of the title and its source, Shakespeare's Sonnet number 111:

> My nature is subdu'd
> To what it works in, like the dyer's hand.

Now his matter is music, and his section is "Homage to Igor Stravinsky," It includes "Notes on Music and Opera," a piece that is both serious and amusing on "Cav and Pag" (*Cavalleria Rusticana* and *I Pagliacci*), a piece on writing opera libretti, done with Chester Kallman, and, finally, an essay on "Music in Shakespeare." This repeats the view dramatized in *The Sea and the Mirror*, that *The Tempest* does not end as G. Wilson Knight and other critics have supposed in total harmony, in the reconciliation suggested by Gonzalo's speech about our all having found ourselves—so that the movement of the play will be from tempestuous discord to musical concord—because only Alonso repents. Elements that have been apparent throughout the collection converge here: the return to Shakespeare, the celebration of musical fun and games, the analytic and at the same time light approach to intellectual and literary questions, the underlying moral and religious theme.

As a critic in prose, Auden constantly displays both a personal style and a poet's imagination. His range of interests is impressive enough to remind one of his master, Goethe.[7] The importance of his critical writing may have been somewhat obscured by his appearing so casual about it, and his reputation as a critic overshadowed by his fame as a poet. Yet it seems fair to describe him as one of the major writers of intellectual and analytical prose—*and* poetry—in his time.

5

Postscript

It may be appropriate to end with a "Postscript": It is a term and a form to which Auden was given. At the same time, there is something arbitrary, if not presumptuous, in this chapter title; the postscripts to Auden's life and work remain to be written. They will be the works on which he has exerted influence.

In fact, every chapter title preceding this might be found misleading. One cannot easily distinguish the poet from the poetry because Auden's life enters into his poetry and because the making of poetry was at the center of that life. Furthermore, the plays, often in verse form and containing lyrics that have been separately published, are not detachable from any other part of the man's work. Finally, the prose criticism alternates with poetic passages, while its objects are, in large part, poetry and poetic theory. There are no watertight compartments in Auden's career; there is no way to isolate the forms and elements because he believed that intelligence and emotion, artfulness and honesty, game playing and moral clarity all had to be members of one community.

Among the last collections that he edited is the "commonplace book" entitled *A Certain World*. He said that it was the nearest thing to an autobiography that he would attempt. It amounts to excerpts, a sizeable number of his favorite passages in both poetry and prose, all from other writers, but with some brief paragraphs he provided as introductions. This literary world is his own certain one, and the reader who wanders through it discovers not only a great deal about his critical taste but also how coherent this whole world is, even though it seems so various and comprehensive. The headings include Acronyms, Aging, Algebra, the Alps, Anesthesia, Brass Bands, Birds, Book Reviews, Calvin, Cats, Chiasmus, Choirboys, Christmas, Death, Dejection, Dogs, Dreams, Easter, Eating, Elegies, Eskimos, Forgiveness, God, Hands, Homer, Humility, Icebergs, Journalism, Kilns, Liturgy, Logic, Madness, Money, Numbers, Owls, Plants, Puns, the Renaissance, Roads, Saints, Spoonerisms, Tyranny, Voyages, and War. The last head of all is Writing. These are all matters of which Auden read with interest, and on which he could write.

Auden's reputation as a writer now appears more secure than it might have ten or fifteen years before his death. The number of critical studies, biographies, and memoirs devoted to him has increased so that his own work along with these accounts of that work and of his life fill a fairly extended library shelf. If one can predict a future reputation, it is possible to suppose that he will continue to be known and anthologized as a major writer of lyric poetry but also, and perhaps increasingly, as an interesting and important poet in dramatic forms, and a very considerable critical intelligence.

When Stephen Spender edited a memorial volume, to which a great many distinguished friends of Auden contributed, the emphasis was largely upon personal history, with a good many anecdotes included. Both the first memorial after his death, at the Cathedral of Saint John the Divine in New York, and the memorial ten years later at the Ninety-second Street YMHA, where Isherwood and a number of other younger poets spoke, were devoted to Auden as poet. In each forum, however, in each reminiscence, there was some sense of the man's personal integrity and, as well, the intellectual integrity of his work in every form.

In every form he undertakes, he is authentically himself, with a recognizable voice. Yet, at the end of that last sec-

tion in *A Certain World,* Auden writes that the poet must
convey an expression not of himself (or any passing moment or aspect of self) but of "a reality common to all" that
he can take pleasure in sharing with others. The last words
of this section are a quotation from Saint Augustine:

> The truth is neither mine nor his nor another's; but
> belongs to us all whom Thou callest to partake of it,
> warning us terribly, not to account it private to
> ourselves, lest we be deprived of it.[1]

For all his recognizable idiosyncracy, Auden is an artist
whose work is intended to be public, not romantically or
cryptically personal; as Edward Mendelson has observed,
he was determined to be a civic, not a vatic, poet.[2] The integrity of his written work derives from its being at once
the expression of a consistently recognizable mind but also
its being devoted consistently to public purpose, seeking to
cultivate the ordinary soil and in some small part, even, to
redeem the time. Wisecracking, naughty, even self-indulgent
at moments, he is at last a religious and moral artist.

Notes

1: Poet

1. Humphrey Carpenter's *W. H. Auden: A Biography* (Boston, 1981) explains why the story of Icelandic ancestry may be true: Auðen is familiar in old Norse literature and is still used as a family name in Iceland. Many of the dates, names, and other pieces of information in this chapter derive from Carpenter's detailed work.
2. See Mendelson's *Early Auden* (New York, 1981), especially pp. xii–xviii.
3. These exist in a 98-page ledger with a label on the front cover reading "Poems—April 1929–March 1930." The verses are all in longhand, which is often difficult and sometimes all but impossible to decipher. (The ledger is in my possession.)
4. On John Layard, see Carpenter, pp. 99ff.
5. Auden appears to have had sketchy ideas for plays, one of which, "The Reformatory," was not completed as planned but developed, in collaboration with Isherwood, into *The Enemies of a Bishop*.
6. See Donald Mitchell, *Britten & Auden in the Thirties* (London, 1981), pp. 89–92. Auden's fine lyric "Underneath the Abject Willow" came out of this Auden-Britten collaboration.
7. The reason, he said, was not that he believed he could hide the truth but that the subject need not be so limited by gender, and, besides, nothing was so boring as being told too much about somebody else's love life.
8. See Carpenter, p. 321.
9. Dorothy Farnan's *Auden in Love* (New York, 1984) suggests, with good reason, that Auden never ceased to love him. As the longtime companion (and later wife) of Dr. Kallman, she was close to Chester and fairly close to Wystan Auden, as

well. At a party one evening, she talked of how men as well as women should take care of their complexions—certainly Auden, with his extremely light and delicate skin, did not. It was then that the cold cream episode described at the end of this chapter occurred. Chester and Dorothy exchanged comic notes and pictures often. Yet the Farnan book, for all her sympathy for Chester Kallman, only revived the interpretation of the younger man's behavior as a betrayal of his mentor: A number of the critical reviews suggested that he was a parasite as well as disloyal. Auden himself maintained that he had great talent and, indeed, that in the later Auden-Kallman collaborations, the libretti in particular, the younger poet was the leading contributor.

10. The letter cited here, an attempt to reassure Dr. Auden that the play is faithful and not flippant, is one of which Edward Mendelson very kindly gave me a copy.

11. Carpenter, observing (p. 363) that Auden defended Pound's work publicly, threatened to leave Random House if it refused to publish Pound. He wrote in the *Partisan Review* that the *Pisan Cantos* deserved the award. Carpenter accepts the virtually universal assumption that Auden strongly favored that award. He was, in public, defending his view that poetry should not be judged on the basis of the poet's politics or ethics; he was also, in the specific defense, standing by his fellow judges. Privately, he thought Pound's poetry as a whole too diffuse and deliberately obscure for him to deserve the highest international prize more than a number of others (he was himself awarded it later); very privately, he wondered if a man whose bigotry and treason so marred, so embittered, his character could achieve the highest poetic integrity. (Yet he would not deny the power of the *Cantos* or the importance of Pound's poetic influence.) He was, no doubt, profoundly ambivalent on the whole matter. Finally, I can give no evidence from public utterance that Auden did vote against Pound. He told me quite clearly that he did, and why; I believed and believe him.

12. The Trillings and Auden were friendly, but when Auden once said that any lover of poetry must love the *Lord of the Rings* and was told, "Lionel Trilling doesn't like it at all," he re-

sponded, "Exactly." He maintained, perhaps perversely, that Trilling, though brilliant, did not care for literature.

13. This passage comes from a letter dated November 9, 1953, which is in my collection.

14. Again, the exclusion of this poem from all the selections of his own work that he edited has seemed to some critics and many readers rather baffling, although, for whatever reason, Auden always had trouble with it.

His acquaintance with Hitchcock was renewed and became a friendship when Auden was Neilson Professor at Smith, where the architectural historian was professor of art.

2: Poetry

1. The first draft is on page 53 of the 1929–1930 manuscript ledger. (The ledger was bought in Berlin, but the later poems in it were written in England.) At the end of the poem is the date, October 1929, preceded by a London location which seems to be Hornton Street, conceivably Haveton Street. It might be Horton, a street that extends north from Kensington High Street, but that seems doubtful, from the handwriting (and several other poems give as place of composition the same address). Carpenter—p. 109—observes that it is uncertain where Auden was living at this period.

    Critics seem to agree that Auden's virtual rejection of the poem could hardly be based on that line about architecture, which in any event has a significance more than literal; as so often in Auden, building becomes person, and landscape is temperament. Fuller and others have suggested that the mature critic and poet found the message of this lyric facile and adolescent, as he found that a "change of heart" is rarely accomplished and then only with difficulty.

2. This line became the beginning of Part II in a series of verses included in the 1930 volume.

    The changes in mood and style, along with consistency in method—the use of landscape—and theme—the individual's being perplexed in his quest for love and a home—are evident in other memorable verses of that still formative period leading up to 1930. One verse is about the earliest "coming down/Into a new valley," the somehow familiar location that is always altered by the seasons. Another reflects on the memory of past evenings, like the here and now and *not* here or now, yet another on the illusion of fixed self-defining purpose, the constant illusion of freedom. The poem later entitled "The Questioner Who Sits So Sly" darkly considers the death of loves and lives, with a grim voice declaring that there is "No promised country." Most, but not all, of the verses composed between 1927 and 1930 were included in the first Faber volume, coming after *Paid on Both Sides;* a few appeared, sometimes in changed form, as parts of later volumes. Some of these early pieces were included in Auden's own selections, and many are in Edward Mendelson's *Selected Poems;* but a fair number are found in certain places and not others, in, for instance, Mendelson's *English Auden* but not his edition of *Collected Poems*. In one instance, Auden used the first line of a poem (in the 1929–1930 ledger) as a sentence introducing a "Statement" (Book I, Part III) in *The Orators:* there, the original manuscript lines,

> Men pass through doors and travel to the sea,
> Stand grouped in attitudes of play or labour,
> Bending to children, raising equal's glass,
> Are many times together, man with woman,

are printed as prose.

3. This section echoes the cadence and the language of "Under Ben Bulben," one of Yeats's last poems, one which anticipates his death. That is, it was written only months before that death and, therefore, only months before this elegy was composed. Auden's very deliberate echoing is perhaps the finest, the most subtle, way for him to pay his tribute.

4. These poems, as well as "Ischia," the verses for Eliot and Williams, and "Precious Five," were published in the 1951 volume *Nones*.

5. The poem was addressed to me because Wystan Auden knew that I was born and grew up in Jackson County, Missouri, in which the metropolis is Kansas City; and he assumed, as most people do, that the area was one of flatlands. (It is not: Inde-

pendence and Kansas City are situated on steep river bluffs, and the latter is the hilliest city in the United States outside California.) The parts of America that Auden had not visited remained for him fantasy lands, in which he could place all sorts of people and lively events. One of his unpublished poems, a light-hearted occasional piece, begins,

I went to a party on Saturday night—
Since Morris had told me it wouldn't be right,
Since Marilyn had added that it wouldn't be fair,
If they gave a party and *I* wasn't there.
It started at eight and went on 'til past three:
What a brilliant display of good looks and esprit!
Dear Ronald (assuming that he were still here)
Alone could have coped with this fête of the year.
They'd mixed up the punch in a real French bidet
(Gin, Pernod and vodka—with a dash of Tokay);
Though the medlars in aspic had neglected to jell,
The brandied bananas were phallic as hell!
There were Donna and Alan, who refused to be cheered
By the appearance of Del in a week's growth of beard;
There was stupid Juanita, very much at her ease,
Discussing Vedanta with two drunk R. C.'s:
There was John, holding forth on the state of his chest;
There was Ada (who *hardly* was decently dressed);
There was Betty in blue jeans—and who else?—let's see—
That girl no one spoke to—and, of course, there was *me*.

After this pastiche on Noel Coward with its allusion to Ronald Firbank, the verses proceed with sexual innuendo—on collecting "filthy pictures" and picking people up in the square, stripping down to nothing but a pink boa, and (the host's) trying for hours to "make" one of the young women at the party—and references to artistic pretension—people discuss Peacock, Saint Paul, Martha Graham, and Olivier. It all ends,

Three A.M.: all the wit and the wine had been spent,
And I made like an Arab and folded my tent—

Oh, I'll never forget, though my hair may grow white,
What goes on in Kansas City on a Saturday night!

6. Spears, in *The Poetry of W. H. Auden* (p. 316) observes that
this is a defense of hyperbole and falsehood in, specifically,
love poems, with Dante on Beatrice as the great example. The
changing to Generalissimo as love object is part of the hyperbole (one can hardly imagine Auden's doing just that). Auden's title comes from *As You Like It*, in which Touchstone
the clown uses the phrase when he explains to Audrey what
"poetical" means, as applied to the verse of love: It is, after
all, exaggeration and pretense. The clown, Auden suggests, is
wise; and he can repeatedly speak of himself as playing the
clown in his roles of poet and teacher.

That Auden was very serious about this seemingly light-
hearted and perverse defense of the poet as liar is indicated
by his careful changes in the text. Comparing the first typescript version with the printed poem, one finds that he has
changed "dull provincial palates" to "crude provincial gul-
lets," "silly sausage" to "public nuisance," has made a good
half-dozen other alterations in the interest of precision, added
two lines at the end of the first verse paragraph, and dropped
six lines at the end of the third, rococo lines that describe a
triumphant passage through a swirl of adoring flowers. (The
first typescript draft is in my possession.)

7. It was Hopkins's apparent lack of reticence, his revealing too
much of his spiritual and (inadvertently) his sexual struggles,
that disturbed Auden. Fuller, Hoggart, and Spears, among
other critics, recognize the influence of Hopkins not only in
Auden's early verse but throughout his career. See, too, my
essay "Auden, Hopkins, and the Poetry of Reticence," *Twentieth Century Literature* XX (July 1974), pp. 165–171. Auden's response to Hopkins's poetry was that it achieved
greatness at its best, frequently by taking chances, but also
that it could be excessively passionate, nakedly personal. He
was the first to write of the homosexual strain in Hopkins—
a matter on which most Hopkins critics now either openly or
tacitly agree—and the first to raise the question of some sa-
domasochism in the poetry (and recent commentators have

less discreetly written of just such a quality in Hopkins's verse). But to declare flatly that the poet who so frequently took his style from Hopkins, who could write an affectionate pastiche/upon him, as when bemoaning the defeats of the Oxford football team that "have fallen, fell, kept falling, fell/ ... poor lovies," felt "antagonism" toward the Victorian master is absurdly simple (and simply absurd). Yet this is what John R. Boly does in his brief note on the two poets for *Hopkins Among the Poets,* ed. Richard F. Giles (Hamilton, Ontario, 1985)—pp. 76–79—citing the pastiche, the review of Phare's book, and "Petition," which in an ingenious but forced reading he presents as a parody of "Thou art indeed just." The one point on which Auden had misgivings about both Hopkins and Donne was their abandoning of reticence in writing about personal feeling and religious experience; in his attitude, interestingly, Auden is closer to the Tractarian poets, including Newman and Keble, than to these greater ones (see, on Tractarian reticence, G. B. Tennyson, *Victorian Devotional Poetry*—Cambridge, Mass., 1981). Feigning in poetry, he thought, was better than telling all.

8. The anecdote was recounted to me by Ann Birstein.

3: Plays

1. Spears regards this as "the most entertaining and rewarding" of the earlier plays; his explication of it is sound and imaginative (*The Poetry of W. H. Auden,* pp. 94–100).

2. Some readers, apparently unaware of the poet's own comment on this piece of writing but recognizing that it was meant as harsh parody in its original context, have objected to its inclusion in the *Collected Poetry.* It has seemed to them that after his conversion Auden reprinted what had first been an attack on falsely "moral" sermons, presenting it now as an affirmation of faith. The confusion is understandable because, without a dramatic setting, the Vicar and his sermon sound even more diabolically plausible, at least until the overdone and very unreticent conclusion.

3. The anxious sense of an old order's being disrupted by a frightening new coming is very much like that expressed in

Eliot's "Journey of the Magi," and makes, as well, a neat parallel and contrast to Yeats's "Second Coming," where the comfortable order is not ancient Judaism but Christianity and the new dispensation is as mysterious as it is destructive.

An especially valuable critique of *For the Time Being* that relates this oratorio to both *The Sea and the Mirror* and *The Age of Anxiety,* with extended reference as well to *The Enchafèd Flood,* is Herbert Greenberg's *Quest for the Necessary: W. H. Auden and the Dilemma of the Divided Consciousness* (Cambridge, Mass., 1968); see, in particular, pp. 118–169. Greenberg is not the only critic to perceive the relationship of these three essentially Christian dramas, but he illuminates the works both individually and as a group by showing how basic to Auden's method and message in each are the challenging ideas of Kierkegaard.

4. No critic has commented on feminism in Auden, and he is not a very specifically or a preeminently feminist writer, any more than he is "macho." Yet these two passages from the plays suggest his respect for women as women, as fellow human beings, not girls or baby bearers. About matters human and artistic he was color-blind, ecumenical, and indifferent to gender. Still, on women writers he held firm views. He was vexed by the exclusion of major women from anthologies and standard editions (in particular, Christina Rossetti; he once said that it was as scandalous as stupid that she was, in the 1950s and 1960s, out of print); he very early recognized Virginia Woolf's genius, and he privately thought Marianne Moore the finest poet writing in America.

5. In Part II, Act I of that vast-ranging masterpiece, Faust shudders as Mephistopheles tells him that he is to be led to meet the primal Mothers; these are forces to be feared as they must be also venerated. Robert Briffault's study on the matriarchal origins of human society is entitled *The Mothers* (1927), possibly with Goethe in mind. Auden admired Briffault's work, as he admired in part the work of the anthropologist's disciple the poet Robert Graves, although he disagreed with Graves's assertion in *The White Goddess* that all religious forces are ultimately maternal. Probably the source of this and similar passages is Goethe alone, the genius to whom in

fact he wished to be compared because of his range and depth. See Humphrey Carpenter, *W. H. Auden: A Biography*, Part Two, Chapter 6, "A Minor Atlantic Goethe" (pp. 389–440).

6. That mode retained its appeal almost to the end of his life. In the 1960s, Auden and Kallman collaborated on translations of dramatic works, first the libretto by Goldoni for Dittersdorf's *Arcifanfano, King of Fools,* then the *Bacchae* of Euripides, which they renamed *The Bassarids,* and which was set to music, again, by Henze, and was more of an operatic success than the *Elegy.* It was after that success that the two were asked to do the lyrics for a proposed Broadway musical version of *Don Quixote,* lyrics which were not commercially appealing enough to be used (the ultimate lyrics in that very silly musical, from another source, were saccharine enough to do nicely). Auden was fascinated by the problem of writing for singers, maintaining that some perfectly good verse could not be sung. He consistently said that Chester Kallman was better than he at this sort of task, and that apparently was not mere modesty but a genuine opinion.

4: Prose

1. See Isherwood's *Lions and Shadows: An Education in the Twenties* (London, 1938), p. 184. Here, as he does elsewhere, Auden combines parody with some substance: The master who delivers this oration may be pompous but he is not altogether a fool when he speaks of "this country . . . where nobody is well." There is an excellent commentary on the tone and intent of *The Orators* in Spears, pp. 45–58.

2. This statement, however, must be read in large part as an ironic hope that is finally deflated. Beginning with the prose version of the 1929 lines of verse ("Men pass through doors . . ."), it seems to promise rewards to all but then concludes with the acknowledgment of the curse that is passed from father to child.

3. *The Poetry of W. H. Auden,* pp. 50–53. Spears suggests that the next book (III), consisting of "Six Odes," may be called "the airman's oratory"; and he argues that the second of

these odes is also a parody of Hopkins's *Wreck of the Deutschland*. The passage on how defeat fell, fell, on the Oxford team occurs here, and certainly the whole poem echoes Hopkins in its style, although it ends not in the clear hope for a nation's conversion but in uncertainty about a group of young men, their fears and their futures.

Auden's several uses of the "airman" in his early verse seems once more to express two contrasting meanings, two urges: the need to ascend, in undertaking a quest, to rise above the dull and accursed terrestrial order, and what must finally be seen as a mistaken, a doomed, drive to excel by escaping the real places with their country work and civic duty. At least one critic, François Duchene, sees Auden himself as "the helmeted airman."

4. See Note 7 of Chapter 2, "Poetry."

5. An interesting thread runs through much of the prose written in that period, the idea of relating if not reconciling religious faith to political creed, Christianity to Communism. There appears to be, already, some need to bring together two sides of his own personality, prayer and praise on the one hand, and, on the other, political activism. Recognizing that a triumphant Communism in the West would hold the Church suspect and probably persecute it, he nevertheless argues that, of all political stances, the Communist has most in common with Christianity. After his conversion, he would retain only the moral firmness of his youthful politics, adapting it to religious purposes in the service of charity.

6. Bawdy it may be, but the intent is serious. This is a reprise of Auden's insistent idea that the deadly coldness of self-absorption is infinitely worse than the unwilled and ordinary weakness of the human flesh.

7 Auden became increasingly absorbed with Goethe in his later years, as he makes clear in the line about wanting to be a minor version of the German master. He thought Goethe rather better on geology than on art, the topic on which he wrote so much, too much for Auden's taste. But grumble as he might about Goethean pomposity, even hypocrisy, he had to declare him "a great poet and a great man." See Carpenter, p. 394.

5: Postscript

1. The passage appealed to Auden because it combined his religious sense of the necessity for communion—"we must love each other" meant for him to share with the other—and his critical insistence upon telling truth. The art of which he most disapproved was dishonest art, not playful, indirect, or even cryptic but distinctly falsified poetry that is designed to impress or startle, not to communicate; and of course his major reason for rejecting some of his own earlier poems was at last simply that they were dishonest.

2. The first pages of *Early Auden* are largely devoted to this distinction, which Mendelson demonstrates as one basic to his whole career, to his early turning away from self-conscious modernism but also to his ultimate rejection of Romantic egoism.

Bibliography

The most nearly complete listing of Auden's works—and the compilers themselves modestly write that they are not certain how much they may have been unable to find of obscure publication—is B. C. Bloomfield and Edward Mendelson, *W. H. Auden: A Bibliography, 1924–1969* (Charlottesville, Virginia, second edition, 1972). The most recent and complete editions of poetry are those edited by Edward Mendelson, *Collected Poems* (New York, 1976), replacing the 1945 *Collected Poetry;* and *The English Auden* (New York, 1977), which includes essays and dramatic works. For a list of major publications, see Carpenter, pp. 459–460. The main collections of manuscript are in the Berg Collection of the New York Public Library, which has the largest and most important holdings; the British Library; the Bodleian Library, Oxford; the Butler Library, Columbia University; the Houghton Library, Harvard University; the Swarthmore College Library; and the Humanities Research Center at the University of Texas. There are also private collections; by far the largest and most important is that of the late Christopher Isherwood.

There are a good many books and shorter pieces that provide information about various phases of Auden's life, including volumes by E. R. Dodds, Day-Lewis, Dorothy Farnan, Isherwood, Charles Miller, Spender, Stravinsky, and Upward. The one full and reliable biography is Humphrey Carpenter's (Boston, 1981), which includes a list of biographical sources (pp. 461–462). Charles Osborne's *Life of a Poet* (New York, 1979), although mostly reliable for facts, is extremely limited and flawed.

The following is a brief list of critical studies.

Bahlice, George W. *The Later Auden* (New Brunswick, N.J., 1970).
On the poetry from "New Year Letter" to *About the House.*

Beach, Joseph Warren. *The Making of the Auden Canon* (Minneapolis, 1957).
Written while the canon was still in the making, this study is still of some value.

Blair, John G. *The Poetic Art of W. H. Auden* (Princeton, 1965).
A fairly short, readable account of the lyrics; Blair believes that Beach gives them a too "neo-Romantic" reading.

Buell, Frederick. *W. H. Auden as a Social Poet* (Ithaca, 1973).
Useful for Auden in the 1930s; Buell overemphasizes the role of political ideas in the work as a whole.

Callan, Edward. *Auden: A Carnival of Intellect* (New York, 1983).
Explores intellectual development but not at the expense of its artistic embodiment.

Davidson, Dennis. *W. H. Auden* (London, 1970).
A short introductory volume.

Duchene, François. *The Case of the Helmeted Airman* (London, 1972).
Argues, interestingly, that only the later work gives coherence to what might, lacking it, seem to be a group of unrelated or wholly ambiguous pieces.

Everett, Barbara. *Auden* (London, 1964).
Concise and critically acute.

Fuller, John. *A Reader's Guide to W. H. Auden* (New York, 1970).
A very useful series of explications, done with critical skill.

Greenberg, Herbert. *Quest for the Necessary* (Cambridge, Mass., 1968).
As the title suggests, this is an account of how the theme of the quest runs through Auden's work; it is an illuminating study.

Hoggart, Richard. *Auden: An Introductory Essay* (London, 1951).
The earliest full critical volume on the poetry and one that remains influential.

Mendelson, Edward. *Early Auden* (New York, 1981).
The value of Mendelson's criticism is not limited to its insight into early poetry, for what he writes is relevant to Auden's development, to the whole body of his work.

Replogle, Justin. *Auden's Poetry* (Seattle, 1969).
A relatively full-scale account of ideas, style, and comic forms in Auden's verse.

Rodway, Allan. *A Preface to Auden* (London, 1984).
Just what the title suggests, somewhat sketchy but useful for context and background data.

Spears, Monroe K. *The Poetry of W. H. Auden: The Disenchanted Island* (New York, 1963).
An excellent critical study, particularly good on the poetic drama.

Wright, George T. *W. H. Auden* (Boston, Revised Version, 1981).
Worth consulting, but more informative than critical.

Index